THE ROAD FROM MONTICELLO

*A Study
of the Virginia Slavery Debate of 1832*

BY

JOSEPH CLARKE ROBERT

1941

AMS PRESS
New York

Reprinted with permission of Duke University Press
From the edition of 1941
First AMS EDITION published 1970
Manufactured in the United States of America

Library of Congress Catalogue Card Number: 70-109912
SBN: complete set: 404-51750-1
volume 24: 404-51774-9

AMS PRESS, INC.
NEW YORK, N. Y. 10003

PREFACE

The Virginia slavery debate of 1832, final and most brilliant of the Southern attempts to abolish slavery, represents the line of demarcation between a public willing to hear the faults of slavery and one intolerant of criticism. It is almost axiomatic that spokesmen for the Southern States at one time freely acknowledged the evils of Negro slavery and at a later period heatedly defended the merits of the system. Though the elusive isothermal lines of slavery opinion may not be plotted with infallibility in all the Southern States for any given date, it seems clear that the revolution in thought came to the principal slaveholding areas about the year 1830.

There is convenient merit in the thesis that Virginia and South Carolina to an appreciable degree set the pattern of ideas for the rest of the South; thus the developments in either of these two states possess magnified importance. South Carolina, with the notable Baptist leader, Dr. Richard Furman, guaranteeing the benefit of clergy, and the even more famous Dr. Thomas Cooper, contributing the language of the freethinking academician, had almost, if not quite, shed the cloak of apology by 1830. In Virginia the ultimate result of the slavery debate of 1832 was to crystallize fluctuating sentiment into an attitude favorable to the permanent retention of the institution. Contemporaries heralded the debate as the first free and full legislative discussion of abolition in the South; in no other gathering below the Potomac did so many political leaders unite to condemn by phrase and by vote their own system of labor. Yet reaction to these sentiments gave currency to defensive arguments that shaped Southern thinking for three decades and more. For confirmation of the point one need only remember the title of Thomas Roderick Dew's bible of the proslavery cause, *Review of the Debate in the Virginia Legislature of 1831 and 1832*.

In a peculiar way the Virginia problem epitomized the slavery controversy of the nation. Almost every argument advanced by slavery advocate and Northern abolitionist from that time to the Civil War was anticipated in the debate of 1832, and the Virginia disputants possessed the advantage of knowing their subject first-hand. As attested by Virginia's division in the 1860's, its smaller sectionalism paralleled the animosity in a larger area. More than a simple difference of opinion, the debate represented a clash between the independent small farmer of the west, depending on few or no slaves, and the larger planter of the east, relying on chattel labor.

The conflict in the forum at Richmond fits into a design broader than sectionalism and slavery. It typifies the perpetual struggle between the radical, crying for experiment, and the conservative, championing the *status quo* and claiming more evil in the remedy than in the disease. Enthusiastic reformers in the debate saw it as one phase of the world liberal movement, as an echo of the efforts in England, France, Belgium, and Poland. The debate in Jefferson's classic building on the James is of intrinsic interest as an exhibition by the educated Southerner in his chosen field of intellectual activity. By its very nature the genius for oratory was but an ephemeral expression of the creative spirit save when the novelty of the occasion demanded record in newspaper or pamphlet. Some of the passages are literary achievements of no mean merit; for their pure euphony they deserve mention in the cultural history of a people.

Such works of the past dozen years as T. M. Whitfield's *Slavery Agitation in Virginia, 1829-1832* (Baltimore, 1930), W. S. Jenkins's *Pro-Slavery Thought in the Old South* (Chapel Hill, 1935), and Clement Eaton's *Freedom of Thought in the Old South* (Durham, 1940) indicate that scholars are appreciating the distinctive value of the speeches made by Virginia legislators in 1832. The purpose of the present essay is to afford a convenient summary of the causes and consequences of the debate, to present evidence concerning the economic interest in the institution of slavery possessed by the members of the House of Delegates, and to provide in the extracts from the debate representative selections from newspapers and pamphlets rarely available to the student. The participants, though narrowly restricted by the modest confines of this volume, are thus allowed to speak for themselves. The least satisfying phase of this work has been the task of selecting statements most worthy of reproduction. Judgment on this point varies not only from person to person, but, it must be confessed, from day to day with the same person.

This study grew out of a seminar exercise undertaken in 1928 under the direction of Dr. William Kenneth Boyd, late Professor of History at Duke University. In a condensed form the conclusions were presented to the Mississippi Valley Historical Association at its meeting in Memphis, April, 1939. The preparation of the present essay was facilitated by the constructive criticism of President Francis Pendleton Gaines of Washington and Lee University, Dean Carl Wittke of Oberlin College, Professor Henry H. Simms of Ohio State University, and Professor Charles S. Sydnor of Duke University.

J. C. R.

Durham, North Carolina
January 2, 1941

CONTENTS

	PAGE
PREFACE	v
CHAPTER	
I. INSURRECTION AND PANIC	3
II. A SEARCH FOR SAFETY	12
III. THE PECULIAR INSTITUTION ARRAIGNED	20
IV. THE TRIUMPH OF CAUTION	29
V. SECOND THOUGHTS AND THE PUBLIC	37
VI. THE TURN TO THE RIGHT	46
APPENDICES	
A. Selections from the Debate	57
B. List of Delegates, Their Votes and Slaveholdings	113
INDEX	119

THE ROAD FROM MONTICELLO

CHAPTER I

INSURRECTION AND PANIC

The crops were laid by in Southampton County, Virginia, by the end of the third week in August, 1831, and, as was their custom, many farmers harnessed their teams, packed up their families, and drove south to the Carolina camp meeting grounds to refresh their souls and to renew acquaintances. This exodus left many neighborhoods in the Black Belt county without their usual quota of white families. In the atmosphere of general relaxation a handful of Negroes, under the leadership of Nat Turner, plotted the bloodiest of the Southern slave insurrections. Turner, slave preacher and prophet who had captured the imagination of his fellow-blacks, interpreted a strange blue cast of the sun as a heavenly sign to begin his mission. In the early morning hours of August 22 he led his armed band over the sleepy countryside. Stimulated by brandy and Turner's energy, the Negroes carried through their assault on the first plantation. After this deed they were driven on by the taste of blood and the knowledge that the time for retreat had passed. That day and the next about sixty whites, most of them women and children, were slain in brutal fashion. Although Turner's "army" grew in size, its numbers probably never exceeded seventy at any one time. Many Negroes, from fright or affection, remained loyal to their masters; conspicuously faithful were the slaves of Dr. Blount, gouty and determined old gentleman who successfully defended his house against the rebellious blacks.

To crush the revolt white men poured into Southampton. Governor John Floyd, after fretting over constitutional difficulties, succeeded in sending four crack companies of the state militia. Federal forces hastened to co-operate. Three companies from the regular army detachment at Fortress Monroe, in addition to sailors and marines from the *Natchez* and the *Warren*, were ordered to Southampton. Fancy-dress society corps from Virginia towns, tobacco-chewing, hard-drinking bands of irregulars from everywhere, including a company from North Carolina, patrolled the affected areas. Perhaps two thirds of the insurgents were shot down; the rest were taken for trial. There were whites as vengeful as the slave rebels; the frenzy of excitement drove restraint from otherwise moderate men. Pure panic and mob spirit during the heat of the chase allowed no fine distinction between the innocent and the guilty, and tales of reckless cruelty might be multiplied. Had not the organized military companies intervened, there would have been even greater destruction. Though "General" Nat plagued his pursuers by eluding them for over two months, the insurrection was effectively broken the second day. Visiting troops soon turned homeward, many of them cursing the predatory keeper of Vaughan's Tavern and his "stinking" food, most of them pondering the bloody week, the endless funerals, the gory black heads posted as warnings.[1]

[1] Contemporary accounts of the Southampton Insurrection may be found in the following journals: *Richmond Enquirer*, Aug. 26, 1831; *Constitutional Whig*, Richmond, Aug. 25, 29, Sept. 3, 1831 (espec. Sept. 3, account by Editor Pleasants himself, who was with the Richmond troops: original issue not examined, but the account was widely reprinted); *Raleigh Register and North Carolina Gazette*, Sept. 1, 8, 1831; *Niles' Weekly Register*, Baltimore, Aug. 27, Sept. 3, 1831; *Southern Religious Telegraph*, Richmond, Sept. 2, 16, 1831. Special phases of the insurrection are clarified in *Baltimore Gazette*, quoted in *Pennsylvania Intelligencer*, Harrisburg, Sept. 3, 1831; *New York Herald* and *Norfolk Beacon*, quoted in *New York American*, daily, Sept. 6, 1831; *Southern Times*, quoted in *United States Telegraph*, Washington, Oct. 4, 1831. Governor Floyd's diary, printed in C. H. Ambler, *The Life and Diary of John Floyd* (Richmond, 1918), and his papers, Virginia Executive Papers (MSS, Virginia State Library, Richmond) yield additional details. Brief but apparently accurate is the report of two military scouts in North Carolina Governors' Papers (MSS, North Carolina Historical Commission, Raleigh), Ser. LXII, Doc. 249. For the narrative of the leader himself there is the pamphlet, *The Confessions of Nat Turner* (Baltimore, 1831), ed. Thomas R. Gray, counsel of Moses, one of Turner's fellow-conspirators. That Gray was counsel for Moses—not for Turner, as some writers have assumed—is proved by the certificates of the Court of Oyer and Terminer, Virginia Auditors' Papers (MSS, Virginia State Library), Box 197. Apparently the *Confessions* may be accepted as an honest attempt to record the condemned Negro's own story. Another pamphlet of the insurrection is that published by Samuel Warner, *Authentic and Impartial Narrative of the Tragical Scene Which Was Witnessed in Southampton County* (New York, 1831). Floyd's gubernatorial message repeated the story of the insurrection; in the House of Delegates it was a favorite theme all during the 1832 debate. Legislative Petitions (MSS, Virginia State Library) by slaveholders asking compensation for Negroes put to death without trial throw additional light on the period of the insurrection. See, for example, Petition No. 9803A, Southampton County, explaining in detail the hamstringing and execution of a slave known as Alfred. Petition No. 10110A (Dec. 10, 1832), Southampton County, describes the demands made on a tavern keeper by some of the troops. The most extensive secondary account of the insurrection is W. S. Drewry, *The Southampton Insurrection* (Washington, 1900), also published under the title, *Slave Insurrections in Virginia (1830-1865)* (Washington, 1900). While not always accurate as to the condition of the country before and after the in-

From Delaware to the far south the slaveholding country was agitated. Wild rumor amplified the truth until men believed the plot was nation-wide. Disturbed citizens in the Cotton States considered legislation which would curb the further introduction of Negroes into their borders. Governor James Hamilton of South Carolina turned his thoughts from nullification long enough to propose to Governor Montfort Stokes of North Carolina and to Governor Floyd of Virginia the possibility of joint remedial measures. Because the center of the revolt was only about twenty miles from North Carolina, that state was almost as agitated by the insurrection as was Virginia. Militiamen near the border were called into service. According to written reports reaching Governor Stokes, three people were literally scared to death in the false alarms which followed reports from Southampton. Nothing less than a detachment of the regular army from Fortress Monroe could quiet the nervous people of New Bern. *Niles' Register* for September 17, 1831, carried an alarmist story of the destruction of Wilmington by the blacks. As in Virginia, Negroes suspected of participation in the conspiracy were the objects of indiscriminate retaliation.[2]

From the time of the insurrection to the present, it has been emphatically affirmed that Turner and his aides were inspired by Northern abolitionists.[3] This explanation of the origin of the out-

---

surrection, Drewry's narrative is valuable for its contemporary accounts of the uprising. S. B. Weeks, "The Slave Insurrection in Virginia, 1831," *Magazine of American History*, XXV, 448-458 (June, 1891), summarizes the event. An unsigned essay, "Nat Turner's Insurrection," *Atlantic Monthly*, VIII, 173-187 (Aug., 1861), recounts the uprising from the insurgents' point of view. Turner is made the hero in W. W. Brown, *The Black Man* (2d ed.; New York, 1863), pp. 59-75. For other sympathetic stories see J. W. Cromwell, "The Aftermath of Nat Turner's Insurrection," *Journal of Negro History*, V, 208-234 (April, 1920); J. C. Carroll, *Slave Insurrections in the United States, 1800-1865* (Boston, 1938), chaps. v-vii. The insurrection is woven into fiction by G. P. R. James in *The Old Dominion or, the Southampton Massacre* (New York, 1856).

[2] North Carolina Governors' Letter Books (MSS, North Carolina Historical Commission), 1831-32; Borgland to Stokes, Sept. 18, 1831; Hawkins to Stokes, Aug. 26, 1831; Spiria to Stokes, Aug. 25, 1831; Whitfield to Stokes, Sept. 12, 1831; Stokes to Hamilton, Nov. 18, 1831; Proclamation, p. 61; Pardon, p. 95. North Carolina Governors' Papers (MSS, North Carolina Historical Commission), Ser. LXII, Docs. 259, 305, 307. J. S. Bassett, *Slavery in the State of North Carolina* (Johns Hopkins University, *Studies*, Ser. XVII, Nos. 7-8, Baltimore, 1899), pp. 96-97.

[3] Governor Floyd's message, House and Senate *Journals*, 1831-32; Governor Floyd's letter to Hamilton, Ambler, *The Life and Diary of John Floyd*, pp. 89-90; Drewry, *Southampton Insurrection*, p. 181; S. A. Ashe and L. G.

break, widely accepted by Southerners of that period, made every literate Negro a threat because he could read incendiary literature, every Negro assembly a danger because pernicious doctrines could be broadcast there. Among legislators it was a convincing argument for new restrictions on schooling and assemblage of slaves. The accusation of Northern complicity has never been proved, however, and it is almost certain that no direct encouragement was given Nat Turner by the abolitionists. Turner seems to have been a self-hypnotized religious fanatic, in whom came to a focus the restless passions of a race condemned to enforced servitude. Although Northern abolitionists later explained the insurrection in terms of Nat's harsh treatment, this claim is contradicted by the testimony of the Negro himself, if one may believe Gray's printed version, *The Confessions of Nat Turner*, which bears the stamp of genuineness as to facts.

Truth to tell, the action of the Garrison abolitionists immediately before and after the insurrection lent plausibility to the belief that they had stirred up the Negroes. The *Liberator* of July, 1831, contained a bit of poetry urging "Africa" to "strike for God and vengeance now." Garrison declared, however, that he had not one subscriber south of the Potomac. After the insurrection the *Liberator* announced that the bloodshed was but "a prelude to the deluge" and spoke of the uprising as the "hour of vengeance." It is not surprising that a correspondent of the Tarboro *North Carolina Free Press* suggested barbecuing of the *Liberator's* editor and distributors if they were ever caught. Several Northern journals saw in the disastrous event the hand of Garrison.[4]

In the North, yet unconverted to abolitionism, the general emotion was sympathy for the South in its distress and fervent thankfulness that the free states were not living under the black cloud of servile revolt. The sorrows of Southampton momentarily dampened

---

Tyler, "Secession, Insurrection of the Negroes and Northern Incendiarism," *Tyler's Quarterly Historical and Genealogical Magazine*, XV, 2 (July, 1933); L. G. Tyler, *The Federal Period, 1763-1861* (*History of Virginia*, Vol. II, Chicago, 1924), p. 463. J. C. Carroll, in his *Slave Insurrections in the United States, 1800-1865*, pp. 126-127, sees a direct connection between the distribution of *Walker's Appeal* and the Southampton Insurrection.

[4] Philip Slaughter, *The Virginian History of African Colonization* (Richmond, 1855), pp. 29-30; [W. P. Garrison,] *William Lloyd Garrison* (New York, 1885-89), I, 238-239; *Washington Daily Globe*, Sept. 23, 1831; *National Intelligencer*, Washington, Oct. 1, 1831; *Pennsylvania Reporter*, Harrisburg, Dec. 13, 1831.

the fires of sectionalism, at this period being fed by the tariff controversy. A Virginian, visiting in Boston at the time of the insurrection, was warmly assured that the people of Massachusetts, no matter what they thought of slavery, would fly to Virginia's aid if the Old Dominion needed help. The editors of the *New York American*, while maintaining their hatred of the institution, declared that in the areas where slavery existed through no fault of that generation of owners, "we would go to the utmost length to sustain the rights and safety of those whom circumstances have placed in the relation of masters." In acknowledging such expressions the Fredericksburg *Arena* informed its subscribers that the Northern newspaper comments were "entirely unobjectionable."[5]

Back in Virginia the public mind remained apprehensive despite soothing assurances that the danger had passed and that the August plot had been merely local. Governor Floyd was troubled by insistent petitions for arms and registered in his diary especial irritation at the "fear, cowardice and alarm" of Norfolk. Petersburg, expecting the war of the races, was thrown into a fright one night when some practical joker blew a signal horn. The temper of the Black Belt hung dangerously near the panic stage, sustained partly by the fact that Nat Turner was at large until October 30. Mutual suspicion clouded all normal race relations. White Baptists in southside Virginia refused to take customary communion with the colored brethren; these, in turn, rejected the administrative and disciplinary control of the church.[6]

Calm faces were but masks worn to deceive the slaves. "The horrors of Southampton have aroused them," wrote a sympathetic

[5] *Richmond Compiler*, quoted in *National Intelligencer*, Nov. 5, 1831; *New York American for the Country*, New York City, Sept. 20, 1831; *Arena*, quoted in *Niles' Weekly Register*, Sept. 17, 1831. See also *New York Evening Post*, quoted in *Washington Daily Globe*, Sept. 23, 1831; *Southern Religious Telegraph*, Nov. 4, 1831.

[6] Floyd's *Diary*, Oct. 17, 1831 (citations from Governor John Floyd's diary printed in Ambler, *The Life and Diary of John Floyd*, will be given in this fashion, by date, for greater clarity); Edward S. Gregory, "A Sketch of the History of Petersburg," in Campbell & Company, *Directory and Gazeteer of the City of Petersburg, 1877-1878* (Richmond, 1877), p. 39; *Minutes of the Virginia Portsmouth Baptist Association. Held at Otter Dams Church, Surry County, Virginia, May the 26th, 27th and 28th, 1832* (Norfolk, 1832), pp. 9, 11, 25-27, 45; Black Creek Church Minute Book (MS, Virginia Baptist Historical Society, Richmond), 1818-62, Sept., 1831, Jan., 1832. For a shrewd interpretation of the whistling-in-the-dark tactics of Virginia editors see *Genius of Temperance, Philanthropist and Peoples Advocate*, New York City, Sept. 7, 1831.

Northerner with respect to the Virginians. "They lie down to sleep with fear. They hardly venture out on nights. A lady told me, that for weeks after the tragedy, she had quivered at every blast of wind, and every blow of the shutter. Bolts and bars were tried, but the horrid fear haunted the whole population day and night. Aye[!] and night was no release from care, but demanded an increase of sentinels. Then came the haggard fantasies of uneasy slumbers, dreams conjuring up frightful shapes, and all the shew of a diseased imagination."[7] There was some slackening of tension when Nat Turner was caught near the scene of the insurrection, tried, and executed. The captor of Turner received $1,100 in rewards; the estate to which Turner belonged, $375, the sum at which Nat was valued; and according to the *Norfolk Herald*, Nat himself, for consenting to eventual dissection, a small sum which he spent for gingercakes.[8]

The impact of the insurrection on Virginia was conditioned by four salient factors in the life and thought of the Old Dominion, which must be reviewed before the events of the following six months can be evaluated: (I) sectionalism, (II) economic stringency, (III) the antislavery tradition, and (IV) dismay at the increasing majority of blacks over whites in eastern Virginia.

(I) An ominous note was the growing antagonism between the eastern and western parts of Virginia. To be sure, there had been friction between coast and back country since the seventeenth century, but the sectionalism of the moment was powered by a force peculiarly characteristic of the Jacksonian generation, the insistent but unsatisfied demands for democracy in state government. It should be remembered that ante-bellum Virginia was by nature divided into four great sections: (1) the Tidewater, from the sea to the fall line; (2) the Piedmont, from the fall line to the Blue Ridge Mountains; (3) the Valley, between the Blue Ridge and the Alleghanies; and (4) the Trans-Alleghany region. The Tidewater and Piedmont, called the east, and the Valley and Trans-Alleghany section, the west, diverged fundamentally in their economic interests. The typical easterner, practicing a plantation economy, produced tobacco with slave labor; the typical westerner raised wheat and live-

[7] Washington correspondent of *Portland Advertiser*, quoted in *Massachusetts Spy*, Worcester, Feb. 29, 1832.
[8] *Norfolk Herald*, quoted in *Constitutional Whig*, Nov. 17, 1831. The certificate of execution and the valuation by Court of Oyer and Terminer are in Virginia Auditors' Papers, Box 197.

stock with free labor. The sections varied markedly in the density of their Negro population. According to the figures in the census of 1830, 56 per cent of the Tidewater population was black, 54 per cent of the Piedmont; the Negroes thus outnumbered the whites east of the Blue Ridge. In the western part of the state there was an entirely different ratio: the blacks constituted only 23 per cent of the Valley population, and only 10 per cent of the Trans-Alleghany section.[9] The west, disgruntled at state policies, especially at the lethargy in providing transportation facilities, felt that all evils resulted from political inequalities which gave the older section, the east, a preponderance in the legislature not justified by the distribution of white people. The Constitutional Convention of 1829-30, on which the west had pinned its hopes, only partially corrected existing evils; the resulting document granted neither manhood suffrage nor a white basis of representation, both features close to the heart of the newly settled regions. The Convention cast the disputes into lasting form and left the Trans-Alleghany district, in particular, a center of complaint.[10]

(II) Virginia in 1831 was afflicted with a case of hard times, a chronic complaint dating from the Panic of 1819. With good reason her people considered the interval since that financial crisis as a dozen lean years. Farmers spoke of their worn-out lands, and by the thousands sought salvation in moving to the virgin soils of the Western States. Competition from the newly peopled areas threw into blackest despondency those planters who, through patriotism, calculation, or inertia, had refused to go. Their lamentations, public and private, testified to a depression frame of mind which invited strange programs of reform.[11]

(III) There was a respected antislavery tradition in Virginia descended principally from the agitations of the Revolutionary period, a time when religious, economic, and political forces encouraged demonstrations against the institution. Believing slavery inconsistent with Christian principles, the Quakers, ably seconded by special

[9] Compiled from the census of 1830 as entered in *Journal of the House of Delegates of Virginia*, 1831-32, Doc. 21.
[10] For the growth of sectionalism in Virginia see C. H. Ambler, *Sectionalism in Virginia from 1776 to 1861* (Chicago, 1910), and *A History of West Virginia* (New York, 1933); J. C. McGregor, *The Disruption of Virginia* (New York, 1922); J. H. Callahan, *Semi-Centennial History of West Virginia* (Semi-Centennial Commission of West Virginia, 1913).
[11] J. C. Robert, *The Tobacco Kingdom: Plantation, Market, and Factory in Virginia and North Carolina, 1800-1860* (Durham, 1938), pp. 140-143.

groups in other denominations, pressed the attack on slaveholding. Recurrent periods of economic stringency caused masters to look at their black wards and to doubt the efficiency of a system which made no abatement in labor costs, even when low prices cried for curtailment of plantation staples. The political theories of the American Revolution spurred antislavery sentiment, for many statesmen held that bonded blacks in kitchens and tobacco fields contradicted those inalienable rights of man presented in the Declaration of Independence. Conspicuous Virginia leaders of the time, Richard Henry Lee, Patrick Henry, George Mason, and George Washington, all showed dislike for the system of slavery, but Thomas Jefferson proved most outspoken and readiest to present actual plans for abolition. With heated eloquence he described the pernicious effects of slavery on Virginia and outlined gradual emancipation schemes providing freedom and deportation for all born after a certain date. At William and Mary College, symbol of intellectual maturity in Virginia, St. George Tucker and George Wythe, professors of law, advocated antislavery doctrines. In 1796 Tucker presented to the Virginia legislature an elaborate emancipation system partly based on Jefferson's earlier *post nati* projects. Wythe, redoubtable signer of the Declaration of Independence, saw no point to colonizing the Negroes, and, in the words of one of his students, "Mr. Wythe, to the day of his death, was for *simple abolition*, considering the objection to color as founded in prejudice. . . ."

While failing in the grand object of state-wide emancipation, these Revolutionary impulses brought about the act of 1778, which barred African slave ships from Virginia ports, and the act of 1782, which provided such a simple process for private emancipation that manumissions in Virginia averaged about a thousand a year for the next decade. The rapidly increasing free Negro population and the Gabriel Insurrection, an abortive attempt in 1800, prompted a decline in Revolutionary humanitarian enthusiasm. The new temper is best represented by the law of 1806, which, renewing a Colonial principle, declared that an act of manumission was illegal unless the Negro left the state. In 1830 there was some concern over the discovery in Richmond of the incendiary pamphlet, *Walker's Appeal*, written by a free Negro of Boston, once a resident of North Carolina. The fear of such inflammatory literature bore fruit in a law which narrowly restricted assemblies held for the purpose of schooling Negroes. Thoughtful citizens everywhere were willing to admit that slavery was of doubtful value to Virginia economy and society, though the subject was no longer considered a proper theme for public declamation. As a humanitarian venture, reputable groups over Virginia supported the American Colonization Society, which, founded in Washington in 1816, soon took for its definite purpose the transplanting of free blacks to Liberia. In June, 1831, the Virginia branch, presided over by Chief Justice Marshall, congratulated itself on the decline of hostility, in the North and South, to the program of the society.[12]

(IV) The newly published figures from the census of 1830 distressed thoughtful Virginians. Prideful orators and practical politicians grieved as they saw their state declining in relative rank. Virginia was first in population as late as 1810, second by 1820, now only third. There would be congressional reapportionment with consequent reduction of power in the House of Representatives and in the electoral college. Even more ominous was the increasing majority of blacks over whites east of the Blue Ridge. In 1790 whites had exceeded blacks by 25,000; in 1800 the preponderance was reversed and blacks outnumbered whites by 3,000; in 1810 by 48,000; in 1820 by 65,000; in 1830 by 81,000. The Southampton Insurrection gave point to pessimists who calculated the public safety of Tidewater and Piedmont in terms of relative numbers in the racial formula.[13]

[12] This survey of early antislavery sentiment in Virginia is based principally on A. D. Adams, *Neglected Period of Anti-Slavery in America, 1808-1831* (Boston, 1908); J. C. Ballagh, *A History of Slavery in Virginia* (Johns Hopkins University, *Studies*, Extra Vol. XXIV, Baltimore, 1902); W. M. Gewehr, *The Great Awakening in Virginia, 1740-1790* (Durham, 1930); M. S. Locke, *Anti-Slavery in America, 1619-1808* (Boston, 1901); J. H. Russell, *The Free Negro in Virginia, 1619-1865* (Johns Hopkins University, *Studies*, XXXI, No. 3, Baltimore, 1913); C. G. Woodson, *The Education of the Negro Prior to 1861* (New York, 1915). The standard work on colonization is E. L. Fox, *The American Colonization Society, 1817-1840* (Johns Hopkins University, *Studies*, XXXVII, No. 3, Baltimore, 1919). The earlier publication, Slaughter, *The Virginian History of African Colonization*, is of interest principally because of the light which it throws on the events surrounding the slavery debate. For the Walker pamphlet and its effect see Clement Eaton, "A Dangerous Pamphlet in the Old South," *Journal of Southern History*, II, 323-334 (Aug., 1936); *Acts of the General Assembly of Virginia*, 1830-31, chap. xxxix, secs. 4-8. The remark concerning Wythe may be found in [B. W. Leigh,] *The Letter of Appomattox to the People of Virginia* (Richmond, 1832), p. 43.

[13] See *Journal of the House of Delegates of Virginia*, 1831-32, Doc. No. 21.

CHAPTER II

A Search for Safety

In the period between the insurrection in August and the meeting of the legislature in December, it was commonly felt that measures should be taken by the General Assembly to prevent a second Southhampton. The public journals carried plans for getting rid of slavery and printed schemes for further repression of the Negroes, aims not always divergent, since some Virginians believed that the Negroes should be freed and sent away, but that in the meantime they should be held in stricter subjection. Apparently no one advanced as a serious proposition abolition without removal of the black race.

Despite the fact that only two free Negroes received formal conviction for participation in the Southampton Insurrection, the class was always suspected of plotting, just as it was charged with petty thievery. This mistrust, re-enforced by the fact that white artisans were jealous of the free blacks' hold on sundry small mechanical trades, led to a clamor for their removal. Thus suspicion and jealousy were superimposed on much altruistic idealism already present in the ranks of the Colonization Society. To some Virginians deportation of free Negroes was the maximum of hope. To others it seemed only the initial step toward riddance of the entire Negro race; the free blacks would go, the slaves would follow. Ultra-conservatives, relishing no scheme which threatened property, proposed stricter police regulations and the driving out of the free Negroes whether they wanted to go or not.

A familiar suggestion was to dismiss annually from the state just enough Negroes to guarantee that the whites would increase faster than the blacks. One group of slaveholders surveyed population statistics and pointed out the startling change in the complexion of eastern Virginia. Remove, said they, at least a fraction of the annual colored increase. One estimate was that state-sponsored exportation of about two thousand Negroes per year would put an end to the danger of insurrections. Special emphasis was given to the consideration of this increasing Negro majority in eastern Virginia by the news that Georgia and Louisiana, disturbed by the Southampton Insurrection, had passed laws to prohibit the introduction of slaves for sale, and that other slave-buying states were planning similar measures to curb the domestic slave trade.[1]

Encouraged by the numerous proposals that Virginia Negroes be deported, officials of the American Colonization Society optimistically looked to the coming legislature for some appropriation. Ex-President James Madison, head of the national organization, believed it a propitious time for beginning the gradual extermination of slavery. Chief Justice John Marshall, president of the Virginia branch, thought the moment favorable for obtaining money from several state legislatures and possibly for laws which would make free Negroes more anxious to emigrate.[2] About two hundred Southampton County free Negroes, encouraged by a series of nocturnal whippings, expressed an earnest desire to be sent to Africa, and sailed before the end of the year on a ship chartered by the American Colonization Society.[3]

The August days brought a new frame of mind to the Old Dominion. Governor John Floyd, statesman-surgeon who owned over a dozen slaves at his Montgomery County home, weighed this human property and found it wanting. He determined that in his administration Virginia would initiate some program of gradual abolition. Before the meeting of the legislature he wrote to Governor Hamilton of South Carolina outlining his plans, which included stricter rules for all Negroes, expulsion of free blacks from the state, gradual purchase and eventual dismissal from Virginia of the slave population.[4] For generations philosophical gentlemen in their closets

---

[1] See espec. *Constitutional Whig*, Oct. 6, 1831; *ibid.*, quoted in *United States Telegraph*, Washington, Oct. 26, 1831; *Pennsylvania Telegraph*, Harrisburg, Dec. 7, 1831. For a survey of the general subject of population prediction as an item in the slavery argument see various articles by J. J. Spengler, espec. "Malthusianism and the Debate on Slavery," *South Atlantic Quarterly*, XXXIV, 170-189 (April, 1935).

[2] *African Repository*, VII, 370-372 (Washington, Feb., 1832), Marshall to Gurley, Dec. 14, 1831, Madison to Gurley, Dec. 29, 1831; Slaughter, *Virginian History of African Colonization*, pp. 58-59.

[3] *Richmond Enquirer*, Oct. 7, 1831; *African Repository*, VII, 285, 320 (Nov., Dec., 1831); William H. Brodnax, *The Speech of William H. Brodnax, (of Dinwiddie) in the House of Delegates of Virginia, on the Policy of the State with Respect to its Colored Population. Delivered January 19* [sic], *1832* (Richmond, 1832), p. 43; *National Intelligencer*, semiweekly ed., Nov. 30, Dec. 24, 1831.

[4] Personal Property Books (MSS, Virginia State Library), Montgomery County, 1831, 1832; Ambler, *John Floyd*, pp. 89-90. On Nov. 21, 1831, Governor Floyd wrote in his diary: "Before I leave this Government I will

had freely condemned the Southern institution, but editors had gingerly skirted the issues. Now the public press willingly presented emancipation schemes which, a half year before, would have been deemed fanatical. In commenting on this fact a liberal slaveholder observed, "A few months have wrought a great change in public sentiment concerning this subject."[5]

With dignity becoming a legislative body over two centuries old, the General Assembly met December 5, 1831, in Richmond. At the north end of the Capitol, the House of Delegates came to order in its accustomed hall, the room in which John Marshall had presided over the trial of Aaron Burr, and in which Robert E. Lee was to accept command of the Virginia army. Of the 134 members of the House, 36 came from the Tidewater, 42 from the Piedmont, 25 from the Valley, and 31 from Trans-Alleghany.[6] A free white basis, computed according to the census of 1830, would have taken six seats from the east (Tidewater-Piedmont) and given them to the west (Valley-Trans-Alleghany). Approximately three fourths of the delegates were slaveholders, though only 18 had the distinction of owning more than 20 taxable slaves, i.e., Negroes over twelve years of age. The average number of slaves held by the delegates from each of the four sections was: Tidewater, 13.7; Piedmont, 14.0; Valley, 3.3; Trans-Alleghany, 1.2. Of the 32 known nonslaveholders, 26 came from the west.[7]

An unusually large number of young men had been successful in the April elections, men more youthful in years and in spirit than the venerable crowd of Revolutionary maturity which had assembled two years before to make a new constitution for Virginia. The new generation possessed such leaders as Thomas Marshall, eldest son of

---

have contrived to have a law passed gradually abolishing slavery in this State, or at all events to begin the work by prohibiting slavery on the West side of the Blue Ridge Mts." See also entry for Dec. 26, 1831. Hamilton, Governor of South Carolina, had written to both Floyd of Virginia and Stokes of North Carolina asking about the insurrectionary movements in their states and suggesting the possibility of joint measures to remedy the situation. For letter to Stokes see North Carolina Governors' Papers (MSS), Ser. LXIII, Doc. 433.

[5] "Mohun" in *Petersburg Times*, quoted in *Southern Religious Telegraph*, Dec. 2, 1831.

[6] J. A. C. Chandler, *Representation in Virginia* (Johns Hopkins University, Studies, XIV, Nos. 6-7, Baltimore, 1896), pp. 42, 44.

[7] From county tax books the taxable personal property, including slaves if any, may be determined for all but ten of the delegates. See below, Appendix, "List of Delegates, Their Votes and Slaveholdings."

John Marshall; Thomas Jefferson Randolph, favorite grandson of Thomas Jefferson; William H. Roane of Hanover, grandson of Patrick Henry; James McDowell, Jr., nephew of Governor Floyd; and William B. Preston, another nephew of Governor Floyd and son of ex-Governor James P. Preston. An even dozen of the delegates eventually went to Congress; some achieved prominence in national politics. McDowell became a member of Congress and Governor of Virginia; Preston became a congressman, and in Taylor's administration Secretary of the Navy; Faulkner was sent to the House of Representatives, became minister to France under Buchanan, served on Stonewall Jackson's staff, and later was elected West Virginia congressman.[8]

On December 6 Governor Floyd delivered his official message surveying the problems confronting Virginia. In the course of his analysis of Federal relations he gave comfort to South Carolinians by condemning the central government, "merely the Agent of the States," for its unconstitutional measures. The men of Columbia were not ungrateful; as a courteous gesture in 1832 they cast their eleven presidential electoral votes for him. The principal topic of Floyd's message was, of course, the Southampton disaster, which the Governor believed to have been incited from neighboring states. He pointed out the danger from Negro preachers, and recommended a revision of the laws to subordinate slaves. Although he suggested that money be appropriated for the removal of free Negroes from the Commonwealth, Floyd did not include any reference to the abolition schemes which had been revolving in his mind.[9] In the House of Delegates on motion of Fisher it was ordered "that so much of the Governor's message as relates to the insurrectionary movements of the slaves, and the removal of the free persons of

[8] In a sense the debate was a revolt of Virginia youth against ancestral restraint. "An Old Virginian," in the *Constitutional Whig*, Jan. 19, 1832, remarked that "the youthful talent of the House has entirely conducted this momentous debate." See also Thomas R. Dew, *Review of the Debate in the Virginia Legislature of 1831 and 1832* (Richmond, 1832), p. 7. The ages of prominent antislavery speakers, determined from their last birthdays, were: Faulkner, 25; Preston, 26; Summers, 27; McDowell, 35; Moore, 35; Randolph, 39. For ages and political careers see *Biographical Dictionary of the American Congress, 1774-1927* ([Washington,] 1928); Allen Johnson and Dumas Malone (eds.), *Dictionary of American Biography* (20 vols.; New York, 1928-36).

[9] *Journal of the House of Delegates of Virginia* (hereinafter cited as *House Journal*), 1831-32, Doc. No. 1; *Richmond Enquirer*, Dec. 8, 1831; *Constitutional Whig*, Dec. 6, 1831.

color beyond the limits of the Commonwealth, be referred to a committee" with leave to report by bill or otherwise.[10] This select committee, appointed with other committees to consider different parts of the Governor's message, had an original membership of thirteen, only three of whom came from west of the Blue Ridge. Since it was a committee to examine the causes of the Southampton Insurrection, at the time it seemed only reasonable to appoint most of its members from the Black Belt.

Delegates presented the usual deluge of resolutions and memorials drawn up by their constituents. Those documents identified by title as relating to the colored population were naturally referred to the select committee appointed to consider that part of the Governor's message which dealt with the same subject.[11] On December 14, William H. Roane of Hanover desired to read two petitions respecting Negroes. He read the first, and began with the second, which was from The Religious Society of Friends. William O. Goode of Mecklenburg, without waiting to hear this petition, moved that both be referred. Roane thought that he should finish reading the document from the Friends. Accordingly, the House of Delegates listened to the memorial from the Quakers, who had been petitioning with some regularity for years in regard to slavery: "We therefore solemnly believe that some efficient system for the abolition of slavery in the Commonwealth and restoration of the African race to the inalienable rights of man, is imperiously demanded by the laws of God, and inseparably connected with the best interests of the Commonwealth at large." Goode, unsympathetic with such notions, reversed his parliamentary position and moved that the House reject the second memorial.

Here ensued a brief forensic skirmish on the subject of slavery, which was but a preliminary to the tournament reserved for January. The main question was whether or not to refer the petition to the select committee. The delegates voted for reference, 93 to 27, though some of the majority pointedly observed that the ballot

---

[10] *House Journal*, 1831-32, p. 15; *Richmond Enquirer*, Dec. 8, 1831; *Constitutional Whig*, Dec. 9, 1831.

[11] Symbolic of the new self-confidence acquired by the women of America in the era of Frances Wright were resolutions submitted by feminine groups asking for relief from the dangers of slavery. See *National Intelligencer*, semiweekly, Dec. 3, 1831; J. C. Carroll, *Slave Insurrections in the United States, 1800-1865*, pp. 153-155. For early petitions asking for the purchase and removal of slaves see *Richmond Enquirer*, Dec. 10, 1831; and remark of Campbell of Brooke, in *Constitutional Whig*, March 20, 1832.

did not force the committee to report agreeably on the petition. From such expressions it is evident that this cannot be considered a test vote. Nevertheless, it is interesting to note that of the twenty-seven opposing this slight concession to antislavery opinion all but two came from east of the Blue Ridge.[12]

Perplexing questions were arising in the select committee, and its members were eager to share both the labor and responsibility of making a report. On December 31 committee chairman Brodnax asked Banks, conservative speaker of the House of Delegates, to appoint eight additional men. After this the committe totaled twenty-one, sixteen of whom were easterners. Faulkner, one of the minority from west of the Blue Ridge, on January 2, 1832, presented to his fellow committee members a resolution declaring for a scheme of gradual emancipation, guaranteeing, however, either retention by owners of slaves then living or adequate compensation for them if taken. This motion the committee tabled.[13]

From the meeting of the legislature to the opening of the debate proper on January 11 the public mind became more restless and unsettled. Antislavery sentiments were freely expressed in memorials to the legislature and in letters to the newspapers. The Virginia press gloried in its break with tradition and proposed open discussion of a subject which had been guarded in former times "with Turkish jealousy."[14] The Richmond *Constitutional Whig* was running what appeared to be a contest to see who could suggest the best scheme for removing the black curse. The January 7 *Richmond Enquirer* came out with a widely quoted editorial:

> It is probable, from what we hear, that the Committee on the coloured population will report some plan for getting rid of the free people of colour—But is this all that can be done? Are we forever to suffer the greatest evil, which can scourge our land, not only to remain, but to increase in its dimensions? "We may shut our eyes and avert our faces if we please," (writes an eloquent S. Carolinian

---

[12] Petitions Presented to the Virginia Legislature (MSS), Docs. 9815, 9815A; J. H. Johnston, "Antislavery Petitions Presented to the Virginia Legislature by Citizens of Various Counties," *Journal of Negro History*, XII, 670-691 (Oct., 1927); *House Journal*, 1831-32, p. 29; *Richmond Enquirer*, Dec. 15, 17, 1831; *Constitutional Whig*, Dec. 16, 1831. Goode expressed his decision to move the rejection of both petitions presented by Roane, but eventually confined his rejecting motion to that of the Quakers.

[13] *House Journal*, 1831-32, p. 74; *Daily National Intelligencer*, Washington, Jan. 5, 1832.

[14] See *Constitutional Whig*, Jan. 12, 1832.

on his return from the north a few weeks ago) "But there it is, the dark and growing evil at our doors—What is to be done? Oh! My God—I don't know, but something must be done." . . . And though we speak almost without a hope that the committee or that the Legislature will do anything, at the present session, to meet this question, yet we say now, in the utmost sincerity of our hearts, that our wisest men cannot give too much of their attention to this subject—nor can they give it too soon.

Conservatives began to worry for fear that something might be done towards emancipation; especially were they concerned at the frequent prophecies of a general debate on the question. Encouraged by Governor Floyd, the younger antislavery spirits were hoping that the subject would come before the House of Delegates. It appears that the Governor's nephews, McDowell and Preston, provided a nucleus around which liberal legislators gathered. Certainly a half dozen, probably many times this number, indicated in private that they favored some kind of emancipation law.[15] On Wednesday, January 11, the proslavery men provoked the very debate which they wished to avoid.

Goode, strong anti-emancipationist, on January 10 had inquired concerning the progress of the select committee. General Brodnax replied in explanation of any apparent tardiness that the committee's very complicated work consisted of two main problems: the removal of the free Negroes and gradual emancipation. Goode then declared that in his opinion the course taken was productive of "dangerous consequences," and that on the morrow he would present a resolution that would save the committee considerable labor.[16] Accordingly, on January 11 he rose and made the following motion:

Resolved, That the select committee raised on the subject of slaves, free negroes, and the melancholy occurrences growing out of the tragical massacre in Southampton, be discharged from the consideration of all petitions, memorials and resolutions, which have for their object, the manumission of persons held in servitude under the existing laws of this commonwealth, and that it is not expedient to legislate on the subject.

But those in favor of emancipation were not to be outdone in a

---

[15] See Floyd's *Diary,* Jan. 9, 10, 11, 1832, and developments in the debate. Note the strong leadership furnished by McDowell and Moore of Rockbridge County, where Floyd practiced his profession of surgery before going to Montgomery County.

[16] *Richmond Enquirer,* Jan. 12, 1832; *Constitutional Whig,* Jan. 13, 1832.

parliamentary way. Thomas Jefferson Randolph countered with another proposition by moving the following Jeffersonian plan as a substitute, to be placed after the word "Southampton" in the Goode motion:

—be instructed to inquire into the expediency of submitting to the vote of the qualified voters in the several towns, cities, boroughs, and counties of this commonwealth, the propriety of providing by law that the children of all female slaves, who may be born in this state, on or after the 4th of July, 1840, shall become the property of the commonwealth, the males at the age of twenty-one years, and the females at the age of eighteen, if detained by their owners within the limits of Virginia, until they shall respectively arrive at the ages aforesaid, to be hired out until the net sum arising therefrom, shall be sufficient to defray the expense of their removal, beyond the limits of the United States, and that said committee have leave to report by bill or otherwise.

These two motions, a motion to compel the committee not to consider abolition and a counter proposal requiring it to consider a specific proposition for emancipation, immediately initiated the debate, which lasted two full weeks.[17] On January 16, in the middle of the discussion, the select committee reported by resolution: *"Resolved as the opinion of this committee,* That it is inexpedient for the present legislature to make any legislative enactment for the abolition of slavery." There was considerable wrangling over parliamentary procedure in the management of the committee report. To simplify matters it was suggested that the committee report be tabled and that the discussion of the Goode and Randolph motions of January 11 be continued. Put in the form of a motion, this plan lost, 60 to 62. There was no special significance to the balloting; individual votes were not even recorded. Technically the committee report was now before the house, and the motions of the eleventh were out of order. Preston moved that the committee report be amended by substituting the word "expedient" for "inexpedient," thereby reversing the report and declaring that some legislation should, at that session, be passed for the abolition of slavery.[18] The maneuvering on the sixteenth did not change the character of the debate; from the eleventh to the twenty-fifth the basic issues before the House remained the same.

[17] *House Journal,* 1831-32, p. 93; *Richmond Enquirer,* Jan. 12, 1832; *Constitutional Whig,* Jan. 13, 1832.
[18] *House Journal,* 1831-32, p. 99; *Constitutional Whig,* Jan. 17, 1832; *Richmond Enquirer,* Jan. 17, 1832.

CHAPTER III

The Peculiar Institution Arraigned

The novelty of publicly discussing slavery in the assembly hall was acknowledged on all sides, by those favoring as well as by those condemning the policy of open doors and full newspaper accounts. Conservatives prophesied dire effects from bandying wild schemes of abolition; they feared, at best, a serious decline in the price of slaves, at worst, a train of new Southamptons. Liberals, breathing the air of a new age of reform, rejoiced that the subject had come from under the old taboo, and applauded the raising of the curtain which so long had veiled the topic of slavery. To them it was a heroic age, and they did not flinch from heroic remedies. Almost bursting with optimism, they were willing to declare with George W. Summers, as he pointed to the acceptance of the Hanover antislavery petition, "This is the act to which after time will trace the origin of American abolition."[1]

The most sensational feature of the debate was the relentless attack made by the would-be reformers on the system of Negro slavery. The institution was denounced as never before; it was condemned in wholesale fashion by legal representatives of a slaveholding people. The vigor and breadth of the assault provide the debate with its most obvious distinction. The principal complaint was that the institution injured the whites, and that the Negroes, as shown by the Southampton Insurrection, constituted a threat to the very lives of their masters. Yet occasional bursts of rhetoric included pleas that liberty was the natural right of the black man.

Among the insistent delegates who had pondered over the natural rights of man as described by Mason in the Virginia Bill of Rights and by Jefferson in the Declaration of Independence was Samuel McDowell Moore, from the county of Rockbridge. On the first day of the debate Moore did not hesitate to issue a broad challenge to slavery:

The right to the enjoyment of liberty, is one of those perfect, inherent and inalienable rights, which pertain to the whole human

[1] For this and subsequent quotations from the speeches see Appendix, "Selections from the Debate."

race, and of which they [the slaves] can never be divested, except by an act of gross injustice . . . slavery is at best, but an intolerable evil, and can never be submitted to, except from stern necessity. . . . Liberty is too dear to the heart of man, ever to be given up for any earthly consideration.

Yet Patrick Henry's grandson, William H. Roane, moderately antislavery in basic tendencies, dismissed the philosophical inheritance of the American Revolution with the bald announcement that he did not "believe in that Fan-faronade about the natural equality of man."

George I. Williams, brilliant nonslaveholder from beyond the Alleghanies, could not restrain himself when John T. Brown of Petersburg denied that the slaves wanted their freedom. After a brief display of sarcasm, he launched into a transcendentalist flight worthy of Emerson: "The poorest tattered negro, who tills the planter's field, under his task-master, and labors to produce those fruits which he may never call his own, feels within him that spark which emanates from the deity—the innate longing for liberty,—and hears in the inmost recesses of his soul, the secret whisperings of nature, that tell him he should be free." And James McDowell in like tone protested that, despite any treatment accorded the slave, ". . . the idea that he was born to be free will survive it all. It is allied to his hope of immortality—it is the ethereal part of his nature which oppression cannot reach; it is a torch lit up in his soul by the hand of the Deity and never meant to be extinguished by the hand of man."

Set against these philosophical gems was the cumulative testimony of the debate affirming the essential mildness of the Virginians in the ordinary administration of their institution. Critics took opportunity to point out certain cruelties, for example, the breaking up of families in the domestic trade and the indiscriminate slaughter of the Negroes in the Southampton panic; but it seems to have been accepted that the treatment of the slave was not such as to cause humanity to weep over his lot. Naturally it was the conservative group which declaimed with greatest enthusiasm the kindly nature of plantation rule.

The typical argument against slavery was that it reacted disastrously on the whites, perverting their social outlook and checking their economic progress. This is what the social critics in the Virginia legislature usually meant when they said that slavery was an "evil." The word, with its sociological and economic implications, should be distinguished from the words "sin" and "immorality," with their ethical concepts. A majority of all speakers agreed that slavery was an evil, and racked their brains in searching for figures of speech sufficiently condemnatory. In handling the tender topic of manners and morals, debaters spared neither poor white man nor plantation magnate. George W. Summers, in his frank and colorful western style, asserted that habits of idleness, sensuality, and fondness for luxuries were encouraged in a slaveholding community. Remembering the airs of imperious white children (or, as a critic later pointed out, a famous remark made by Jefferson on the same subject), he charged that a slave population exercised "the most pernicious influence upon the manners, habits and character, of those among whom it exists. Lisping infancy learns the vocabulary of abusive epithets, and struts the embryo tyrant of its little domain." Echoing other reformers, Charles J. Faulkner declared that the presence of the slaves created "that unfortunate state of society in which freemen regard labor as disgraceful." This distaste for manual labor, commented Moore, was forcing young men into the already crowded professions.

Antislavery men blamed slavery for all the economic ailments of Virginia, and the charges could be made with spirit since the Old Dominion was languishing under the spell of an enervating depression. Almost as a unit, the liberals maintained that slave labor cost more than free labor, that as laborers slaves were inferior to a free, intelligent population. Henry Berry, a slaveholder himself, asked, "What stimulus has the slave to work, other than the lash?" After listening to a week of debate, James McDowell asserted that he had heard no one question the thesis that in the Virginia latitude the labor of the free white man was more productive than that of the slave.

Slavery was found guilty of oppressing free labor, destroying the hardy class of Virginia "yeomanry," the small freeholder, the honest and industrious but poor laboring man. Such accusations signified recognition of the new political role played by the lower middle class, many of whom had been enfranchised under the Constitution of 1830. It was Chief Justice Marshall's son Thomas, with perhaps $10,000 invested in slaves, who said that slavery was indefensible "Because it is ruinous to the whites—retards improvement—roots out an industrious population—banishes the yeomanry of the country—deprives the spinner, the weaver, the smith, the shoemaker, the carpenter, of employment and support. . . . The master has no capital but what is vested in human flesh; the father, instead of being richer for his sons, is at a loss to provide for them."

So great was the blight of slavery, its critics contended, that whites were emigrating by the hundreds and thousands. In itself this migration left the state in a precarious economic position, but another and a more fateful aspect of the exodus was that it contributed to the increasing discrepancy between the number of blacks and the number of whites in eastern Virginia. As already remarked, the 1830 census had been recently published, and the figures alarmed Virginians, especially since it appeared as though the little overflow of blacks then going south, six thousand or so a year, would be banked up by restrictive laws in the Cotton States. Antislavery political economists, in presenting the estimates of Negro increase, did not rest with a mere statistical survey based on the decennial census returns, but gave a scientific flourish to their argument by demonstrating with Malthusian terminology the contrast between the natural checks on the increase of the whites and the general absence of such retarding influences on the part of the slaves. With the increase in the black majority, all the evils and dangers of slavery would experience corresponding multiplication. The most dreaded result of the mounting black percentage, it was thought by the antislavery group, would be frequent insurrections. Never again would any feeling of security exist when slaves were around; always there would lurk the possibility of returning home to discover wife and child murdered.

Virginia was declining, she was losing her place among the states, and the worst was yet to come, such was the theme of the antislavery group. A favorite device, and one which a quarter of a century later probably gave inspiration to Hinton R. Helper, a close student of the debate, was to compare statistically and graphically Virginia with the free states of the North and West.[2] Over and over again enemies of the slave system painted in heavy nocturnes the run-down condition of Virginia. "In the May-day of life," said Samuel M. Garland from the county of Amherst, "she wears upon her countenance the evidence of premature decay, and the yellow leaf of Autumn has followed too soon the budding blossoms of Spring. And to what known cause can this be assigned, but to the existence of slavery,—this cancer which destroys at the fountain, the streams of vigorous and healthful existence?"

And, finally, critics charged that the system created political dif-

[2] See below, p. 54, n. 18.

ferences within the state and nation. William M. Rives saw in slavery the cause of dissensions in the state over such diverse objectives as internal improvements and a public school system. In explanation of the last point he accused slaveholders of trying to keep poor whites ignorant so that they would not question the institution of slavery. James McDowell complained that slavery caused national dissension, and pessimistically suggested the possibility of a dissolution of the Union. Prophetically he saw the isolation of the South in such an event, since the slaveholders *"will and can coalesce with no other interest."* Thomas Jefferson Randolph's somewhat similar tone is perhaps an echo of his grandfather's old-age despondency over national sectionalism.

To the calendar of evils prepared by the reformers, conservatives presented a variety of answers. Leaders of the group tended to minimize the deficences of the system, but, as will be noted more particularly later, their strategy was concentrated on attacking as impracticable all plans for emancipation. In common with some of the moderate reformers, they dismissed the abstract question of the violation of the natural rights of man and pled the legal support of state and Federal constitutions. In particular James H. Gholson, Alexander G. Knox, and John T. Brown resented the description of the social ill effects of slavery, and would concede no shortcomings in the chivalry, morality, and patriotism of the Virginians. Concerning the inherent economic weaknesses of the institution, the conservatives had comparatively little to say, though some denied the somber descriptions given "good old Eastern Virginia," by those who, according to Gholson, were "better poets than planters." Goode saw the beginning of better ploughing and crop rotation and ascribed the confusion to prices, not production. John E. Shell countered the emigration argument by admitting the movement but questioning the cause. "Not, sir, I assure you to escape the evil and curse of slavery. The emigrant, so far as my observation extends, almost invariably settles again among a slave population. . . ."

Several conservatives would not be satisfied with the negative approach of their friends and openly questioned the thesis that slavery was an evil. Brown and Goode touched on the historical-Bible argument for conservatism, but it was Knox who most openly developed the positive-good theory. This Mecklenburg County delegate, who apparently owned no slaves, declaimed:

I cannot force my mind, even by calling to its aid, humanity, religion or philanthropy, to the conclusion that slavery, as it exists in Virginia, is an evil. But, Sir, on the contrary, I consider it susceptible of demonstration that it is to this very cause, that we may trace the high and elevated character which she has heretofore sustained; and, moreover, that its existence is indispensably requisite in order to preserve the forms of a Republican Government.

Such arguments introduced a new era in the South.

The typical conservative of the Virginia House of Delegates either avoided commitment on the merits of the institution of slavery or admitted deficiencies in the system but insistently returned to the question of ways and means of abolition. Why call slavery an evil, he would ask, when it has become so woven into the Virginia pattern as to be ineradicable? Why agitate the question when no feasible plan has been presented, and can never be prepared? In tabulating the evils of slavery the reform group presented a united front; at the formulation of concrete plans for relief there was diversity of opinion in the antislavery party, and the conservatives had their inning. The unanimity of the liberals in condemning the evil was matched by the unanimity of the conservatives in condemning the remedy. The reformers admitted the immaturity of their plans; they pled that the select committee be instructed to prepare some comprehensive program. They did suggest several general abolition proposals, all of which included deportation of the blacks; no one promoted a scheme for freeing the Negroes and retaining them within the borders of Virginia. All significant formulas for emancipation were developed from the essential ingredient of gradualness. The *post nati* idea certainly had that quality; there was nothing precipitate about a program which gave freedom only to those born after a certain date.

Among the plans suggested for relief from the threatened black deluge was the proposal that Negroes equal in number to the annual increase be moved to Africa. The free Negroes would go first; privately emancipated or state-purchased slaves would follow. Conservatives readily took up the idea of deporting the free Negro, but were displeased with the plan of purchase in any form. A typical scheme advanced by moderate antislavery men was to obtain purchase and colonization money from the Federal Government. Income from the sale of public land, much of which had once been claimed by Virginia, seemed to be the most feasible source of revenue. As might have been expected, Thomas Marshall sponsored this nationalistic idea, a revival of the Rufus King proposal. When such plans were advanced, the slavery men occasionally expressed doubts as to the generosity of the Federal Government and always slipped into an energetic defense of State rights, declaring that aid of this nature would provide the entering wedge for further expansion of Federal powers within the province of the state. State purchase, according to the conservatives, had little virtue because the slaveholders would be merely buying their own property from themselves; they would suffer taxation to provide for this expenditure.

Randolph's proposal, embraced in his substitute motion of January 11, involved intolerable features, according to its critics. The suggestion of a popular referendum on the subject was revolutionary and contrary to the established representative system. The *post nati* principle of emancipation was illegal in that under the common law of *partus sequitur ventrem* the slaveowner had as much right to the offspring as to the slaves actually *in esse*. In making logical deductions from this maxim, Gholson maintained that children from slave mothers, like foals from mares, must be considered as property. Indeed, said this Brunswick County slaveholder, Virginia's wealth was in her slave increase, a statement which provoked a storm of impassioned protest. Conservatives sought to minimize the Jeffersonian characteristics of the Randolph plan by contrasting Jefferson's theory with his practice.

The basic question in the debate, and one which every plan had to answer explicitly or inferentially, was the nature of property rights in the slave. This problem was discussed from all points of view; from the moderate premises of the Randolph motion, which had nothing to do with the slaves then living, to the extreme assumptions in any scheme for immediate abolition by simple state decree. Many reformers temperately acknowledged the validity of the bonds holding the enslaved blacks, but others, by elaborating the superior claims of public welfare, reduced the legal basis of slavery to the vanishing point.

In an early edition of the "higher law" doctrine, determined antislavery men appealed to laws more fundamental than the literal text of written constitutions. George W. Summers of Kanawha advanced the theory that "all property is held subordinate to, and only as it promotes the general welfare of, the community in which it exists." Samuel M. Garland and others elaborated the thesis that the safety of the people is the supreme law. James McDowell, Governor Floyd's nephew, presented the most extensive defense of the right of the state to take property if the well-being of the people demanded it. "The rights of private property and of personal security exist under every government, but they are not *equal*. Security is the primary purpose for which men enter into government; property, beyond a sufficiency for natural wants, is only a secondary purpose." Yet he would not take present slaves from their masters, but would apply his doctrine to the future increase. Attempting to stay within constitutional boundaries, several advanced the theory that slavery existed only by virtue of statute law, which might be repealed; others gave interpretations of the state constitution to show that emancipation plans were compatible with both letter and spirit of the document.

The doctrine of property rights elaborated by McDowell and others infuriated the slavery men who grew rich in sarcasm over the "New Light politicians," bitterly laughed at the strange interpretation, called it revolutionary, cited constitutions and statutes, and threatened civil war if any such idea were incorporated into a plan of emancipation. Willoughby Newton, undoubtedly thinking of his twenty-nine adult slaves at home, cried in desperation that he would just as soon try to convince "the midnight assassin, that my life is my own—or the highway robber that my purse is my property" as to attempt to convert abolitionists to the idea that his slaves were his property. William O. Goode, whose motion of January 11 was in part responsible for the initiation of the debate, asked the day before the final voting, "Is it possible for gentlemen to suppose, that this can be accomplished in peace?" No feasible system of abolition had been or could be presented, contended the conservatives, who added that even if the plans were practicable there were many reasons why emancipation programs should not be adopted at that session. In their desire to delay action they were joined by a group of antislavery men who felt that they should consult their constituents.

Because in general the west condemned slavery and the east condemned the emancipation projects, the debate was studded with evidences of that sectionalism which thirty years later resulted in a division of the state. At first mention of the slavery question in December, members from west of the Blue Ridge made courteous gestures towards the great slaveholding section, so agitated by the insurrection and apparently considering measures to relieve itself from the danger of a recurrence of the tragedy. But the west, given inadequate representation in the key select committee, regretted its impotence when the problems of the committe broadened. William B. Preston, of the minority party in the committee, shouted, "We will be heard." The Valley and Trans-Alleghany delegates denied the easterners' assertion that the question was one which concerned only their section. Soon the Negro population, greatly increasing, would overflow into the western part of the state. John C. Campbell and other western delegates favored a separate state rather than the introduction of the evil into their communities. To refute the westerners' contention that slavery would come to them, Brown of Petersburg, in language which might well have been in Webster's mouth on March 7, 1850, showed that the western "farmers and graziers" would never buy any quantity of slaves. "The foot of the negro delights not in the dew of the mountain grass."

CHAPTER IV

THE TRIUMPH OF CAUTION

The delegates may be divided roughly into three groups: (1) the emancipators, about sixty members who desired immediate action favorable to some plan of abolition; (2) the slavery party, about sixty members who believed that no move should be made towards abolition, some saying that slavery might be an evil but that difficulties in the way of removal were insurmountable; and (3) holding the balance of power, the compromisers, about a dozen who apparently favored eventual emancipation, and certainly wanted an immediate antislavery declaration, but desired postponement of a decision on positive legislation. On Wednesday, January 25, 1832, the debate was concluded by four polls of importance.[1] The first was on a motion to postpone indefinitely both committee report and Preston's amendment, measures which had been advanced on January 16. Vincent Witcher, Pittsylvania County slaveholder who made the motion, explained it as a test vote: those opposed to emancipation legislation would vote *aye*, those advocating antislavery plans would vote *no*. Witcher said that in this manner he would like "to obtain the vote of each member, pro and con, on the question of abolition." His interpretation of the motion apparently went unchallenged, and the slavery group was defeated on the postponement measure, 60 to 71.[2]

The next vote was on Preston's amendment declaring it "expedient" for that legislature to pass enactments for the abolition of slavery—the strongest antislavery motion of the debate. Under the

---

[1] There was, in addition to the four votes here outlined, a vote on postponement to March 31, which was defeated. A record of this is in the *Constitutional Whig*, Jan. 28, 1832, but is in neither the official *House Journal* nor the *Richmond Enquirer*. The record of the voting on Jan. 25 is based on the *House Journal*, 1831-32, pp. 109-110; *Richmond Enquirer*, Jan. 26, 28, 1832; *Constitutional Whig*, Jan. 28, 1832.

[2] *Richmond Enquirer*, Jan. 26, 1832. Wood of Albemarle was the only delegate who opposed postponement and all antislavery measures. See Appendix, "List of Delegates, Their Votes and Slaveholdings." The *Constitutional Whig*, Jan. 28, 1832, maintained that Witcher's motion was the test question, and showed "a majority of 11, who by that vote, declared their belief that at the proper time, and in the proper mode, Virginia ought to commence a system of gradual abolition."

DENSITY OF COLORED POPULATION IN VIRGINIA, 1830

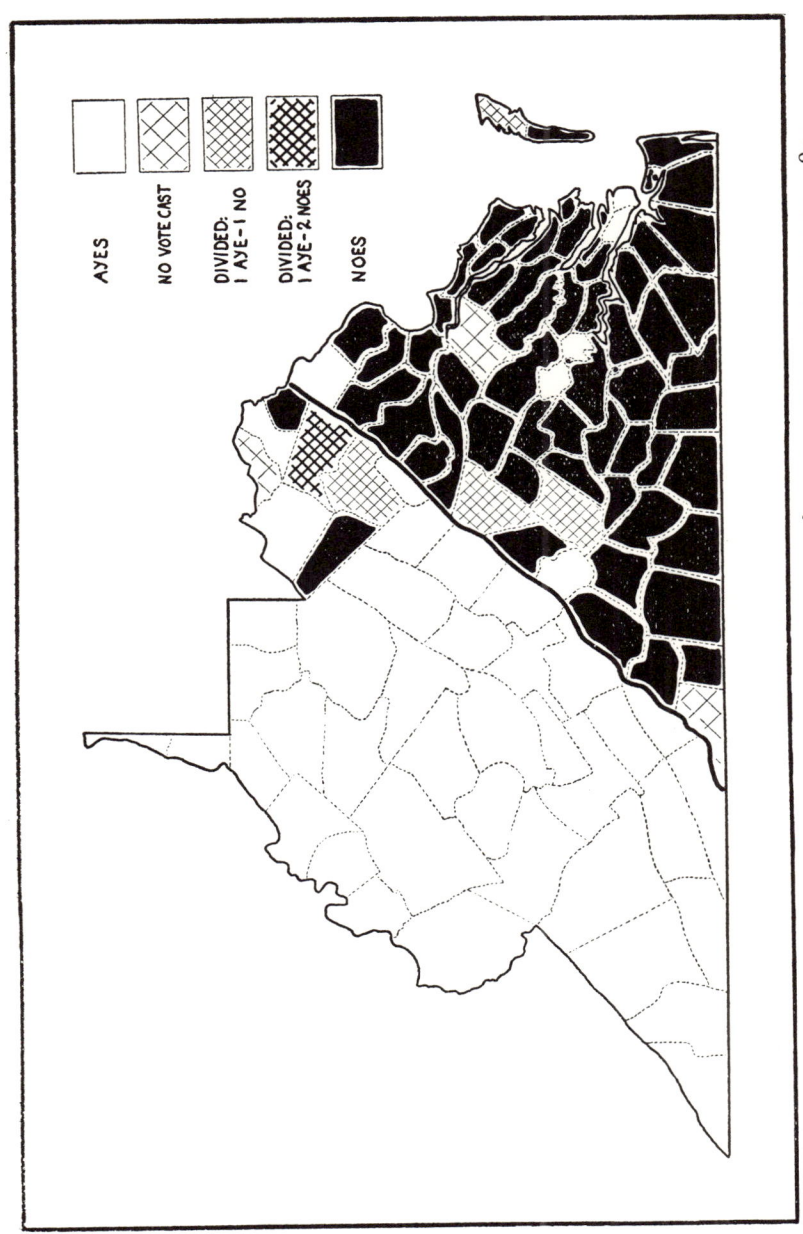

GEOGRAPHICAL DISTRIBUTION OF VOTES ON PRESTON'S AMENDMENT, JANUARY 25, 1832

rules this had precedence over the committee report to which it was ostensibly an "amendment," actually a reversal. The slavery men, supported by the compromisers, defeated the move, 73 to 58.[3] Men in the group of compromisers explained that they feared haste would ruin the antislavery cause.

This development clearly indicated that those for immediate action were doomed to defeat and showed that Bryce's preamble to the committee report was the most vigorous pronouncement against slavery which could be officially obtained. The preamble, which had been advanced by Bryce on the sixteenth but withdrawn on the promise that he would be allowed to submit it later,[4] declared that slavery was an evil, but that action other than the removal of free Negroes should await the further growth of public opinion, especially since the deportation of free blacks would absorb all available funds. The slavery delegates opposed this concession, but, supported by both compromise and antislavery groups, it passed, 67 to 60.

Though the slavery delegates would have favored the original report, the preface composed by Bryce was so offensive that they determined to record their disapproval of the combination. Accordingly, they held their ranks, and the new question of preamble united with the committee report passed by the slim majority of five, 64 to 59. This count was subsequently changed to read 65 to 58 in the official records, as Marshall claimed to have misunderstood the motion.[5] The combined preamble and the committee report then read:

Profoundly sensible of the great evils arising from the condition of the colored population of this commonwealth; induced by humanity as well as policy to an immediate effort for the removal in the first place, as well of those who are now free, as of such as may hereafter become free; believing that this effort, while it is in just accordance with the sentiments of the community on the subject will absorb all our present means; and that a further action for the removal of the slaves should await a more definite development of public opinion, *Resolved as the opinion of this committee,* That it is

---

[3] Of the 58 endorsing this antislavery resolution at least 29 were slaveholders. However, these represented the ownership of only 172 taxable slaves out of the more than 1,100 owned by all members.

[4] *Richmond Enquirer,* Jan. 17, 1832.

[5] The revised figures, 65 to 58, are in the *House Journal,* 1831-32, p. 110. The original vote of 64 to 59 is given in the *Richmond Enquirer,* Jan. 26, 1832. The change of vote is recorded in the *Richmond Enquirer,* Jan. 28, 1832, and in the *Constitutional Whig,* Jan. 28, 1832.

inexpedient for the present legislature to make any legislative enactment for the abolition of slavery.

The votes showed characteristic sectional alignments. In general, the west was for some scheme of abolition, while the east, with prominent exceptions, was for obstructing any such move. On the so-called "test" vote, Witcher's move for indefinite postponement, eastern delegates cast for dismissal of the subject 56 of their 76 ballots, while the western delegates gave to the same cause only 4 of their 55. When Preston's amendment calling for immediate action was presented, the easterners mustered against the motion 67 of their potential 76; the westerners, on the contrary, allowed only 6 negatives in their 55 votes. As demonstrated by the appended table, "List of Delegates, Their Votes and Slaveholdings," similar divisions followed the other motions. A majority of that decisive faction, the compromisers, came from the Tidewater-Piedmont.[6] It is noteworthy that the 58 who opposed the committee report prefaced by Bryce's compromise declaration owned approximately three times as many slaves as the 65 who favored the motion.[7]

At this point it may be remarked that a bill for deporting free Negroes, which included an appropriation of $35,000 for the year 1832 and $90,000 for 1833, passed the House on February 16 by a vote of 79 to 41, but was rejected in the Senate on March 10 by an 18 to 14 vote for indefinite postponement.[8] The Senate accepted various amendments before it finally dismissed the bill. When the

---

[6] The east-west rancor was projected into the consideration of other subjects. A bill for certain internal improvements was defeated by members from east of the Blue Ridge, who said "that they had no interest in such improvements and in revenge for the debate on the negro subject of abolition" (Floyd's *Diary*, Feb. 3, 1832). Ambler states that "The bitterness engendered by this debate was long remembered in both the east and the west. Later it was a factor in the dismemberment of the commonwealth of Virginia and the formation of West Virginia" (*A History of West Virginia*, p. 235).

Even if the west had been given full representation on a free white basis, it appears that the movement of the immediatists in the House of Delegates would have been unsuccessful, though the majority against Preston's amendment would have been reduced from fifteen to approximately eight. This computation is based on the assumption that voting in a reformed house would have followed the sectional alignment indicated in the balloting of Jan. 25, 1832.

[7] See Appendix, "List of Delegates, Their Votes and Slaveholdings."

[8] *House Journal*, 1831-32, p. 158; *Constitutional Whig*, Feb. 18, 1832. Senate voting of March 10, 1832, recorded in *Journal of the Senate of Virginia*, 1831-32, pp. 169-170; *Richmond Enquirer*, March 13, 1832; *Constitutional Whig*, March 13, 1832.

proposed act came from the House, it carried a clause which made possible the application of the appropriation, not only to those Negroes who "voluntarily consented to remove," but also, when and if all applicants of that type were provided for, to those Negroes who might be manumitted for the purpose of coming under the act.[9] Even before discarding the rest of the bill the Senate eliminated the provision for those freed in the future, and also trimmed the 1833 appropriation from $90,000 to $50,000.[10] It is according the colonization bill unwarranted importance to consider its defeat a tragic blow to the antislavery side. Contemporaries saw no such significance in the event.[11] There is convincing evidence that this effort to rid Virginia of her free Negroes was not considered in either chamber as distinctly an antislavery measure. Of the 41 negatives given the bill in the House of Delegates, 23—over half—came from the group that had favored Preston's amendment, the clearest antislavery declaration of the session; again, these 41 negatives were divided 26 from the west and 15 from the east, the slaveholding section. Of the 18 who joined to quash the bill in the Senate, 11 came from the west and only 7 from the east.[12]

There is a persistent legend that a proposition to free the Virginia Negroes was defeated in the 1831-32 legislature by a one-vote margin. A common version has it that the colonization bill, shaped to lead Virginia out of slavery, was lost in the Senate by the difference of a single vote. There are several facts which nullify the various one-vote myths: in the first place, a vote on emancipation as such was never polled; in the second place, the colonization bill, even had its accompanying appropriations been less meager, hardly would have induced manumissions on such a scale as to make any appreciable dent in the slavery system (as noted above, it was not generally con-

[9] The most accessible copy of the bill as passed by the House may be found in *Journal of the Senate of Virginia*, 1831-32, Appendix, Bill No. 2.

[10] *Journal of the Senate of Virginia*, 1831-32, pp. 152, 166.

[11] Cf. Virginius Dabney, *Liberalism in the South* (Chapel Hill, 1932), p. 98. As noted below, exaggeration of the importance of the colonization bill was often united with the one-vote legend. Cf. Fox's thesis that something helpful would have been done for colonization in the 1829-36 period had it not been for the opposition of the east (*American Colonization Society*, pp. 169-170).

[12] It should be remarked, however, that the *Constitutional Whig*, March 13, 1832, suggests that the western senators voted against the bill because they did not want their constituents taxed for transportation costs. Note T. M. Whitfield, *Slavery Agitation in Virginia, 1829-1832* (Johns Hopkins University, *Studies*, Extra Vol., New Ser., X, Baltimore, 1930), pp. 111-112.

sidered an antislavery measure); in the third place, and most conclusive, on no question which could be called a final measure in reference to slavery was the balloting in either chamber as close as one vote. The misconception as to the disposition of the colonization bill in the Senate possibly had its origin in the fact that on March 10 the upper house by a vote of 15 to 16 refused a substitute shaped as an amendment to the colonization bill; this result is recorded in the Senate *Journal* immediately before the vote on postponement.[13] The Senate *Journal*, the *Richmond Enquirer*, and the *Constitutional Whig* concur in the 18 to 14 record for indefinite postponement of the actual bill.[14]

As was usual in Southern legislatures convening subsequent to insurrections, the Virginia Assembly before its adjournment on March 21, 1832, revised the Negro code by restricting still further the liberties of the blacks. The new restraints included the silencing of Negro preachers, strict regulation of night religious assemblies, and a general contraction of the free Negroes' legal privileges.[15] As if to balance the score, the legislature indirectly condemned the retaliatory measures in Southampton by refusing payment for slaves shot without

---

[13] As noted above, there was a 62 to 60 result in the House of Delegates on Jan. 16, but the question was merely one of parliamentary procedure and so insignificant that the names of voters were not required (*House Journal*, 1831-32, p. 99). A 15 to 15 vote in the Senate which rejected an amendment to Section V of the Free Negro Bill eventually was accepted, 17 to 13 (*Journal of the Senate of Virginia*, 1831-32, pp. 148, 166).

[14] The error of the one-vote legend is pointed out by A. B. Hart, *Slavery and Abolition, 1831-1841* (*The American Nation*, Vol. XVI, New York, 1906), p. 177, and by Whitfield, *Slavery Agitation in Virginia, 1829-1832*, pp. 94, 113. With some variation it is related as authentic by Thomas Nelson Page, *The Negro: The Southerner's Problem* (New York, 1904), p. 14; Beverly B. Munford, *Virginia's Attitude Toward Slavery and Secession* (New York, 1909), p. 47; J. H. Latané, *A History of the United States* (New York, 1918), p. 310; Edward Channing, *A History of the United States* (6 vols.; New York, 1905-25), V, 143-144; Landon C. Bell, *The Old Free State* (2 vols.; Richmond, 1927), I, 495-496; James Truslow Adams, *America's Tragedy* (New York, 1934), pp. 97-98. Latané's version is that the select committee, by a one-vote majority, reported adversely on Randolph's plan. Channing wrote under the avowed influence of William Cabell Bruce, who furthered the one-vote legend in his *Below the James: A Plantation Sketch* (New York, 1918), pp. 152-153. In respect to the numerical vote on the colonization bill the one-vote story is accepted by S. E. Morison and H. S. Commager, *The Growth of the American Republic* (New York, 1930), p. 418.

[15] *Acts of the General Assembly of Virginia*, 1831-32, chap. xxii. See also *ibid.*, chap. xxi, authorizing special patrols east of the Alleghany Mountains. See *Constitutional Whig*, March 5, 1832, for a stirring editorial in opposition to more extreme measures directed against the free Negroes.

trial. This rejection of slaveholders' petitions for indemnity was a salutary combination of economy and justice and a guarantee against recklessness in the future.[16]

The central interest in the session, however, was neither the effort at an appropriation for colonization, nor the additions to the black code, but the debate on abolition. After its close, the speeches seemed insipid, and the gallery dwindled.[17] More important than any other resolution or any statute loomed the declarations of the House of Delegates on January 25, at the end of the slavery debate. The editor of the Richmond *Constitutional Whig* interpreted these as follows:

> The enquiry and discussion then, have terminated in the following specific and implied declarations on the part of the House of Delegates: (1) That it is not expedient at this session, to legislate on abolition. (2) That the coloured population of Virginia, is a great evil. (3) That humanity and policy in the *first place*, demand the removal of the free, and those who will become free (looking to an extensive voluntary manumission). (4) That this will absorb our present means. (5) (Undeniable implication) That when public opinion is more developed; when the people have spoken more explicitly, and the *means* are better devised, that it is expedient to commence a system of abolition. The House of Delegates have gone this far, and in our opinion, it had no right to go farther.[18]

---

[16] See Petitions Presented to the Virginia Legislature (MSS), Southampton County, 1831.

[17] "Since the Termination of the discussion on Abolition, the proceedings of the House of Delegates have been flat and insipid" (*Constitutional Whig*, Jan. 31, 1832).

[18] *Ibid.*, Jan. 28, 1832.

It is a striking fact that Joseph C. Cabell, Jefferson's close friend and cofounder of the University of Virginia, a man well versed in the art of political strategy, remained silent during the debate and voted with the ultraconservatives on every ballot.

CHAPTER V

SECOND THOUGHTS AND THE PUBLIC

The debate on a subject formerly tabooed in legislative halls excited tremendous interest all over Virginia. In Richmond the wheels of ordinary business idled as men in shops and countinghouses, flour mills and tobacco factories, heard public proposals for revolutionary social and economic changes, and breathless rumors of pending conflict and state division. Despite the severe weather, visitors crowded the classical capitol building, mute monument to eighteenth-century Jeffersonian ideas now being tested in the cauldron of practical politics. Conspicuously in attendance were the women of Richmond, who felt that they were something more than idle spectators. Had not their sisters in the countryside helped bend the opinion of hardened politicians with delicately worded petitions praying for relief from the evils of slavery? Their presence occasioned gallant plays to the gallery and held tempers at least below the point of actual explosion. All in all, it was a show dear to the heart of a generation treasuring spirited oratory. The spectators were enraptured by the exhilarating mixture of statistics, metaphors, and classical allusions. Some listeners were certain that the eloquence equaled that of Athens' best days; others, less sympathetic, grew sarcastic about the rhetorical nosegays plucked by the younger gentlemen of the House.[1]

Before the final voting of January 25 the delegates were subjected to influences less assuring than those immediately previous to the beginning of the debate. Extravagant language from both sides fretted the moderate mind. Angry retorts by those who saw their slave property threatened convinced easy-going men that nothing drastic should be done until their constituents had been consulted. Governor Floyd, formerly the inspiration of the antislavery delegates, became alarmed at the clashes in the House, especially at the private threats of state division, and decided that the debate "must be checked in erratic tendencies."[2] If letters to delegates followed the

[1] Slaughter, *Virginian History of African Colonization*, p. 64; Floyd's *Diary*, Jan. 20, 1832; "Roane" in *Richmond Enquirer*, Jan. 19, 1832; "A Planter" in *ibid.*, Jan. 31, 1832; *Constitutional Whig*, Jan. 17, 1832.

[2] Floyd's *Diary*, Jan. 21, 1832. Note also entry for Jan. 24, 1832.

trend of those addressed to the Richmond papers, anti-emancipationist voters were putting new pressure on their representatives. Editorially the *Whig* and *Enquirer* of Richmond showed less enthusiasm when the discussion began in earnest. As already remarked, the *Enquirer* on January 7 was for some positive and apparently immediate legislation on slavery. Before the debate ended, that journal began praising the middle course taken by General Brodnax.[3] The *Whig* had less ground to yield. It declared for abolition, but not at that session, and before the debate was over, hoped that the legislature would go no further than Bryce's preamble, refuge of the compromisers.[4] Every prominent Virginia editor applauded the movement to overthrow slavery, but urged caution in planning and gradualness in executing the design.[5]

In the free states the Virginia antislavery movement aroused amazement and hope. Southern leaders, legislators and journalists, were candidly voicing criticisms of their society and economy unthinkable a scant half-year before. Utilizing the labor-saving journalistic device of shears and pastepot, Northern publishers reprinted column after column from Richmond, Petersburg, and Norfolk papers, editorials as well as accounts of the speeches. In Ohio and Pennsylvania, the free states bordering on Virginia, the novel Southern movement was a common topic of conversation.[6] Philadelphians in particular remembered Virginia's tradition of primacy and marked with care the stages in the debate, for they believed that where Virginia led the other slave states might soon follow.[7] The Northern

[3] *Richmond Enquirer*, Jan. 24, 1832. Conservative easterners denounced with particular heat the *Enquirer's* antislavery stand. It is possible that some of this opposition stemmed from a grudge held against the editor, Thomas Ritchie, for his reform agitation previous to the Convention of 1829-30. See C. H. Ambler, *Thomas Ritchie: A Study in Virginia Politics* (Richmond, 1913), chap. v, "Reform and Nullification."

[4] *Constitutional Whig*, Jan. 21, 24, 1832. The *Whig* of Jan. 21 gave the large slaveholders a notable scolding: "We say it again—the large slave holder will at last, be left alone to combat for slavery, against united Virginia. The small slave holder, the yeomanry, the mechanic, the merchant, the youth of the country, will ultimately, combine to remove it."

[5] For notes in regard to the attitude of the *Charlottesville Advocate, Norfolk Herald, Lynchburg Jeffersonian,* and *Petersburg Intelligencer,* see *Richmond Enquirer,* Jan. 19, 1832; *Southern Religious Telegraph,* Richmond, Jan. 27, 1832; *Constitutional Whig,* Jan. 28, 1832. Newspaper endorsement of antislavery ideas was a common point of reference in the debate.

[6] Note the report made by the editor of the *Political Arena* as a result of an extensive tour within a month after the debate (*Constitutional Whig,* Feb. 28, 1832).

[7] For this point see *The Friend, A Religious and Literary Journal,* Phil-

spirit in general was friendly and congratulatory. One citizen from above Mason and Dixon's line felt that no matter what the immediate outcome, the debate was the most glorious act in Virginia history since the Declaration of Independence.[8] The signs of the times pointed to the dawning of a new era, rejoiced a New Englander, who noted with satisfaction the changing attitude of the South with regard to the discussion of slavery.[9] The defeat of proposals for immediate action was interpreted as only a temporary check in the cause of reform.[10]

Attentive Northerners could not escape the conspicuous similarity between the sad pictures drawn by the Virginia debaters to show the blighting effect of slavery, and the equally doleful scenes sketched in Congress at the very same moment by Senator Robert Y. Hayne to demonstrate the impact of the tariff on the South. In debating Henry Clay's motion for tariff modification according to protectionist pattern, the South Carolinian on January 16, 1832, bore witness for his section. "But I assure the gentleman that the condition of the South is not merely one of unexampled depression, but of great and all-pervading distress." "Fields abandoned; the hospitable mansions of our fathers deserted; agriculture drooping . . . ," such was the toll levied by the protective system on South Carolina, said the famous orator.[11] "It cannot be doubted, however, from the facts already stated in the Virginia debates, that the tariff at least, has not been so injurious to the industry of the South as the existence of slavery," rejoined the New York *Courier & Enquirer*.[12] The Richmond *Constitutional Whig* took up the idea and soon rephrased it in words that echoed from factory town to factory town. According to an editorial of February 2, only eight days after the close of the debate, of the ills Hayne enumerated one half should be credited to "rhetorical flourish, and a southern imagination"; three fourths of the remainder

---

adelphia, Dec. 24, 1831; *National Gazette and Literary Register*, Philadelphia, Jan. 21, 1832; *Poulson's American Daily Advertiser*, Philadelphia, March 2, 1832. Pennsylvania interest in Richmond developments arose in part from fear that Virginia free Negroes would come in large numbers to Pennsylvania (*Massachusetts Spy*, Worcester, Feb. 1, 1832).

[8] "Penn" in *Poulson's American Daily Advertiser*, Jan. 27, 1832.
[9] "Suggester" in *Boston Courier*, semiweekly, Feb. 13, 1832.
[10] See *National Gazette and Literary Register*, Jan. 28, 1832; *National Intelligencer*, thrice-a-week, Jan. 19, 1832.
[11] *Register of Debates in Congress*, VIII (1833), Part I, p. 80.
[12] Quoted in *Constitutional Whig*, Feb. 2, 1832; *Poulson's American Daily Advertiser*, Jan. 27, 1832.

to slavery, which caused manual labor to be despised. "It is not a political, but a moral cause, which is at the bottom of southern decline."[13] This dragging in of the tariff question, perhaps inevitable because of special developments in national politics at the time, served no ultimate good purpose; rather, it tended to identify the Virginia antislavery party with a political and economic group unpopular in the planting section.

In Maryland the public followed with sympathetic interest the Virginia contest, though editors took occasion to chide their brethren across the bay. Hezekiah Niles in his Baltimore *Register* was acridly unsympathetic, fairly gloating over the admission by Richmond papers that slavery, not the tariff, was the cause of Southern depression.[14] Maryland journals enjoyed contrasting the great Virginia debate and its results, legislatively sterile except for new police regulations, with the passage by the Maryland legislature of a handsome appropriation for colonization.[15] Incidentally, the eminent scientist, Professor Benjamin Silliman of Yale, delivering a Fourth of July address, in 1832, considered the actions of both legislatures as memorable in history for their declarations that slavery was an intolerable evil.[16]

Necessarily sensitive to any political development of consequence, the national capital was aware of the unprecedented effort in Virginia. The halls of Congress echoed the struggle on the James when Daniel Jenifer, Representative from Maryland, remarked the agitation of the Negro question in his own state and in Virginia and attempted to revive a plan for Federal appropriations to subsidize the colonization of free Negroes.[17] The reaction of two Virginia Congressmen, both of whom proved conscious of the Richmond drama, is suggestive of the attitude of their constituents. Richard Coke, Jr., from Tidewater, on January 24 protested against any

[13] Widely quoted in the North. For example, see *National Gazette and Literary Register*, Feb. 7, 1832; *Massachusetts Yeoman and Worcester Saturday Journal and Advertiser*, Worcester, Feb. 25, 1832; *Greenfield Gazette & Franklin Herald*, Greenfield, Mass., Feb. 28, 1832; *Massachusetts Spy*, Worcester, Feb. 29, 1832.

[14] *Niles' Weekly Register*, Feb. 18, 1832. For general interest see *Political Arena*, quoted in *Constitutional Whig*, Feb. 28, 1832.

[15] *Niles' Weekly Register*, March 31, April 7, 1832; *Annapolis Republican*, quoted in *Richmond Enquirer*, March 30, 1832, and in *Niles' Weekly Register*, April 7, 1832.

[16] *African Repository*, VIII, 169-170 (Aug., 1832).

[17] *Register of Debates in Congress*, VIII (1833), Part II, pp. 1537, 1626-1627.

enlarging of Congressional power and borrowed from his friends' arguments in Richmond by proclaiming the unimportant nature of the Turner Insurrection.[18] A week later Robert Craig, from the western part of Virginia, looking beyond the immediate terms of the Jenifer proposal, presented the problem of slavery itself and declared "that the rights of persons are superior to the rights of property." ". . . shall we make a vigorous and noble effort to rescue ourselves from impending destruction?" he asked.[19]

Perhaps no man in Washington was more interested in the outcome of the debate than Chief Justice John Marshall, whose eldest son, Thomas Marshall, was one of the more conservative antislavery delegates. In Richmond during the early weeks of the legislative session, the Chief Justice was familiar with the first stages of the agitation in the General Assembly. Marshall and Justice Joseph Story, both of whom had come to Washington for the January term of the Supreme Court, visited ex-President John Quincy Adams on January 29, 1832, four days after the decisive votes ending the debate. Adams was told that the debate had been closed by a postponement of the proposal for gradual emancipation, though the vote, with a majority of about twenty, was in favor of rejecting the resolution. Marshall explained, no doubt suggesting the attitude of son Thomas, that several who had voted against the resolution were individually in favor of it, but wished to find out the sentiments of the people. Adams duly recorded the visit in his diary.[20]

Among the characters in Washington giving special attention to the debate was Duff Green, editor of the *United States Telegraph* and ex-member of Jackson's Kitchen Cabinet. Green devoted more than a column of editorial comment to the Virginia slavery debate, which he believed to be "equally unwise and dangerous, not to use even stronger expressions." Any economic decline, insisted this man who had given his daughter in marriage to the son of John C. Calhoun, was principally chargeable to the tariff, not to slavery. "Those who have agitated this subject now, have incurred a weighty responsibility for which they will be held accountable to the people."[21]

[18] *Ibid.*, pp. 1628-1629.
[19] *Ibid.*, pp. 1674-1675.
[20] C. F. Adams (ed.), *Memoirs of John Quincy Adams* (12 vols.; Philadelphia, 1874-77), VIII, 463. For Marshall's continued interest in the Virginia situation and his theory that the state should ask aid of the central government see his letter to E. C. Marshall, Feb. 15, 1832, in A. B. Magruder, *John Marshall* (Boston, 1888), p. 261.
[21] *United States Telegraph*, Washington, Jan. 26, 1832.

Pleasants of the Richmond *Whig* suspected Green of political motives, especially of attempting to convert the apprehensions of the moment into a Calhoun-for-president movement. Though the paper later tempered its tone, the *Whig* declared with respect to Green's editorial, "We have discovered an evident purpose to array the whole South on this question, and to direct the excitement to Mr. Calhoun's advancement."[22]

Citizens in the Western tobacco states showed immediate interest in Virginia's attempt; some gave outspoken approval. The Knoxville *Register* sensed the Virginia mood even before the meeting of the General Assembly and wished success to the antislavery cause.[23]

North Carolina journalists followed a general policy of giving only brief news items and noncommittal editorial notices concerning the Richmond debate.[24] Their lukewarmness is explained in part by the energy of North Carolina conservatives, who rallied to check any sentimentalism as early as December 22, 1831. Gathering under the auspices of the Nash Humane and Slave Protecting Society, newly organized in the heart of the Black Belt, they listened to a keynote address which presented the thesis *"slaves as property"* (legal, historical, and religious aspects of the question), attacked the Methodist Church for its desire to teach the Negroes to read, and criticized both foreign and domestic intermeddlers.[25]

The theme of the Nash Humane and Slave Protecting Society sounded familiar enough in some Southern latitudes, especially in South Carolina, hotbed of nullification, where ultraconservative opinion on the slavery question had been maturing for about a decade. In so far as they were informed of the Virginia proceedings, most South Carolinians disapproved of the antislavery demonstration.[26]

[22] *Constitutional Whig*, Feb. 2, 11, 1832.

[23] Eaton, *Freedom of Thought in the Old South*, p. 173; *Political Arena*, quoted in the *Constitutional Whig*, Feb. 28, 1832.

[24] See *Carolina Observer*, Fayetteville, Jan. 24, 31, 1832; *North Carolina Spectator and Western Advertiser*, Rutherfordton, Feb. 4, 11, 1832; *Western Carolinian*, Salisbury, Feb. 20, 1832; espec. *North Carolina Free Press*, Tarboro, Feb. 7, 1832, notable for the unusual space devoted to exchanges referring to the debate. Among the few North Carolinians converted to a liberal point of view by the Virginia debate was Daniel R. Goodloe, who later moved north of the Potomac and wrote antislavery pamphlets (Eaton, *Freedom of Thought in the Old South*, pp. 252-253).

[25] *Raleigh Constitutionalist*, quoted in *North Carolina Free Press*, Tarboro, Jan. 31, 1832.

[26] For suggestions see *New York Courier*, quoted in *Poulson's American Daily Advertiser*, Jan. 27, 1832; Eaton, *Freedom of Thought in the Old South*, pp. 173-174.

There were exceptions, to be sure. Among them was Joel R. Poinsett, well-known diplomat and anti-Nullifier, who welcomed the news of the brilliant speeches. Somewhere in the Carolinas, Poinsett announced to his French traveling companion, Alexis de Tocqueville, later famous as the author of *De la Démocratie en Amérique*, that there was new enlightenment on the subject of slavery and, in proving his point, cited the movement in the Virginia legislature.[27] The general attitude of the Cotton States towards the emancipation debate is more accurately represented by the pronouncement of the *Southern Recorder*, of Milledgeville, Georgia: "But we have believed, and still believe, that the *less* that is said upon this subject (at least in our own State) the better...."[28]

At the conclusion of the debate numerous expressions in local assemblies and public journals of Virginia opposed the antislavery utterances in the House of Delegates. Citizens of Mecklenburg County met to proclaim themselves *"enemies even unto death"* of all "who shall directly, or indirectly, undertake to rob us of our property, in our slaves, by word, act or deed—nor will we be wheedled by any insidious promise of compensation which shall be offered."[29] In the newspapers, which continued the debate for two or three months under the inevitable noms de plume of the day, the slavery men were now presenting their arguments more frequently and more lengthily than the emancipators. "A.B.C.," for example, dismissed the matter thus:

Sir, I am the advocate of slavery and presume it needless to give the *why* and *wherefore*.

This one thing we wish to be understood and to be remembered —that the Constitution of this State, has made Tom, Dick, and Harry, property—it has made Polly, Nancy, and Molly, property; and be that property an evil, a curse, or what not, we intend to hold it.[30]

The antislavery element was now on the defensive, trying to allay the suspicion resulting from the legislative declarations. "Quietus" assured "our Lords of the Woolheads" that the advocates of

---

[27] G. W. Pierson, *Tocqueville and Beaumont in America* (New York, 1938), p. 652.
[28] Quoted in Eaton, *Freedom of Thought in the Old South*, p. 173.
[29] *National Gazette and Literary Register*, Philadelphia, Jan. 31, 1832.
[30] *Constitutional Whig*, April 13, 1832. The richest example of the illiterate proslavery attitude towards the debate is the letter to the editor of the *Richmond Enquirer*, printed in that journal March 1, 1832.

abolition should not be called "Garrisons" and "fanatics" just because they were mistaken in thinking that a majority of Virginians would take a liberal view of the subject.[31] A neat essay in behalf of the free Negro appeared over the signature "Bacon's Quarter Branch." With deft movements of his pen, the author flayed those who would force the free Negro to leave Virginia. He reduced their arguments to absurdities; then, with a touch perhaps too light in a sledge-hammer era of journalism, he blandly indicated the convenience of having the free Negroes as scapegoats for all unsolved crimes and explored in some detail the practice of miscegenation, which, he insisted, would be complicated, if not imperiled, by the removal of free Negro women.[32]

The most famous of the post-debate newspaper writers on the slavery side was "Appomattox," identified as Benjamin Watkins Leigh, a Richmond lawyer who had distinguished himself politically as leader of the eastern faction in the Convention of 1829-30, and who took his place socially as a member of the select group which pitched quoits, ate barbecue, and drank punch with John Marshall. A slaveholder himself, Leigh was by conviction and by economic interest a most unyielding conservative. His letters to the *Richmond Enquirer,* soon reprinted in pamphlet form, reviewed the debate and decried the "unmanful panic" exposed in the antislavery arguments. He saw no possible plan for abolition and deportation, and advanced the predestinarian thesis that Providence sent the slaves, Providence imposed on the Virginians the necessity of retaining them and keeping them in subjection, and "Providence, in its own good time, will dispose of them and us according to its wisdom." By ingenious innuendo, then less subtle display, Leigh charged that Summers's most eloquent passage was based on Thomas Jefferson's *Notes on Virginia.* As for Jefferson himself, that god of Virginia democracy was damned by faint praise and frank criticism. In character, said Leigh, the man of Monticello was estimable, but he "entertained some odd opinions" and his "Embargo and Restrictive System" "was the prime cause and origin of that *decline* (as it is called) of the southern Atlantic States, and particularly Virginia, which our orators seem to take a sort of melancholy pleasure in discoursing of and exaggerating." On the other hand, Edmund Burke, from whose essay on the French Revolution Leigh had been accused of borrowing, was complimented for "his profound political sagacity." Leigh

[31] *Constitutional Whig,* Feb. 21, 1832.
[32] *Ibid.*

warned his readers that if another insurrection broke out, it would be attributable to neither the Negro fanatics nor the incendiary writings from the North, "but to measures proposed and to speeches delivered, in our own legislature, published and disseminated by our own public journals." Though "Jefferson" in the *Richmond Enquirer* made free with Leigh's "long-winded essay," and the *Constitutional Whig* editorially claimed that he had been out-argued by mere striplings in the legislature, Leigh found a receptive audience among the eastern conservatives preparing to dispute the re-election of any delegate who had favored abolition during the 1831-32 session.[33]

Indeed, the spring elections gave a disheartening blow to the hopes of the antislavery group in Virginia. In the campaigns some of the champions of the *status quo* called their opponents "Negro-lovers" and passed around stories that the men who, at the preceding session, had been for abolition were now in favor of giving the Negroes the ballot. Apparently the more heated campaigns were waged in the east. Although some of the eastern antislavery delegates, Randolph for example, received re-election, Bolling and others were defeated because of their stand on the Negro question. Goode and Knox, slavery leaders in the debate, were returned by large majorities in Mecklenburg County.[34]

[33] Leigh's letters were printed in the *Richmond Enquirer*, Feb. 4, 28, 1832, and reprinted in pamphlet form under the title, *The Letter of Appomattox to the People of Virginia* (Richmond, 1832). In connection with Leigh and his letters see *Richmond Enquirer*, Feb. 16, 1832; *Constitutional Whig*, Feb. 7, 1832; Wm. H. Macfarland, *An Address on the Life, Character and Public Services of the late Hon. Benjamin Watkins Leigh* (Virginia Historical Society, Richmond, 1851); *Dictionary of American Biography*, XI, 152-153; A. J. Beveridge, *Life of John Marshall* (4 vols.; Boston, 1916-19), IV, 76-78, 592; Personal Property Books (MSS), City of Richmond, 1831 (when he owned seven taxable slaves), 1833 (when he owned eight taxable slaves). Apparently because the pamphlet edition of *The Letter of Appomattox* appeared about the time the debate speeches were assuming pamphlet form, B. W. Leigh has been erroneously considered one of the debaters. See Reverend O. Scott, *An Appeal to the Methodist Episcopal Church* (Boston, 1838), pp. 81-84; H. R. Helper, *The Impending Crisis of the South: How to Meet It* (New York, 1860), pp. 202-204, 209-212.

[34] *Constitutional Whig*, April 10, 20, 24, 27, May 1, 1832.

CHAPTER VI

THE TURN TO THE RIGHT

One obvious result of the slavery debate was to stir the Virginia conservatives into formulating defensive arguments. Brown, Gholson, Goode, Knox, and others in the legislature, and Leigh as an observer had made a beginning, yet those opposed to abolition still lacked a masterful survey based on general historical and philosophical principles as well as on the specific circumstances in Virginia. Before the end of the memorable year 1832 the *American Quarterly Review* of Philadelphia published an article in which the author announced that since the Virginia legislature had publicly discussed the question of abolition, "we shall therefore waive all considerations of a prudential character which have heretofore restrained us, and boldly grapple with the abolitionists on this great question." The unsigned essay was written by Thomas Roderick Dew, thirty-year-old professor, who was presenting to the students of William and Mary College a course in history, perhaps the most comprehensive offered by any American college at the time. Dew enlarged his exposition into a pamphlet of seventy thousand words, *Review of the Debate in the Virginia Legislature of 1831 and 1832*, published first in Richmond in 1832, subsequently reprinted under the title *An Essay on Slavery*, and still later bound as one section of the collection, *The Pro-Slavery Argument*. For a third of a century this essay was the manual of Virginia conservatism.[1]

[1] "Abolition of Negro Slavery," *American Quarterly Review*, XII, 189-265 (Sept., 1832); *Review of Pamphlets on Slavery and Colonization* (2d ed.; New Haven, 1833); *Richmond Enquirer*, Nov. 23, 1832; *Constitutional Whig*, Feb. 7, 1832; A. P. Upshur, "Domestic Slavery," *Southern Literary Messenger*, V, 677 (Oct., 1839); L. G. Tyler, *Williamsburg, the Old Colonial Capital* (Richmond, 1907), p. 188; H. B. Adams, "The College of William and Mary," U. S. Bureau of Education, *Contributions to American Educational History*, Vol. I, No. 1 (Washington, 1889), pp. 54-55; B. D. R. Midyette, Jr., "Thomas Roderick Dew," *John P. Branch Historical Papers of Randolph-Macon College*, Vol. III, No. 1 (Ashland, Va., 1909), pp. 5-13; *Dictionary of American Biography*, V, 266-267. Since it was the general policy of Robert Walsh, editor of the *American Quarterly Review*, to omit the names of his contributors, there is nothing significant about the fact that Dew's article was unsigned (F. L. Mott, *A History of American Magazines, 1741-1850*, New York, 1930, p. 276). Dew appears to have acquired a slave only a short time before composing his essay. Personal Property Books

Dew's closely reasoned thesis, curiously enough, was prompted by his antislavery friend, Governor John Floyd. After the debate Floyd became absorbed in national affairs and, in April, 1832, wrote Professor Dew, calling his attention to the subject as mooted in the House of Delegates. The outcome was the *Review,* which Floyd accepted as the final word on slavery.[2]

The Williamsburg savant erected his structure, a landmark of proslavery literature, on a broad foundation of historical and philosophical observations; he compounded his mortar of divine determinism and political localism; he braced his beams with the precepts and practices of notable characters, both ancient and modern. The treatise written by the German-trained professor of political economy, history, and metaphysics was divided into preliminary observations and three major parts. The introduction encompassed a brief résumé of the insurrection and the debate, and the basic thesis "that every plan of emancipation and deportation which we can possibly conceive, is *totally* impracticable." Then, remarking that slavery had been pronounced by its opponents as contrary to the law of nature, Dew, in Part I, *"Origin of Slavery and its effects on the progress of Civilization,"* produced by way of refutation a liberally documented history of slavery.[3] The generalizations were seasoned with references to specific items in Holy Writ and to the general benevolence of the Deity. Frankly advocating the merits of bonded servitude, Dew wrote, ". . . we have no hesitation in affirming, that slavery has been perhaps the principal means for impelling forward the civilization of mankind." In dealing with the origins of slavery in the United States, Dew presented a most disarming criticism of the slave trade—its effects on the natives in Africa and in the *middle passage.* This admission is explained by his contention that the American colonists protested against the slave trade, "that slavery was

---

(MSS), Williamsburg, May 24, 1831, no taxable slave; April 14, 1832, one taxable slave.

[2] For connection between Floyd and Dew see Ambler, *John Floyd,* p. 92; Floyd's *Diary,* Oct. 24, 1832. It is possible that Floyd was subjected to conservative influences from South Carolina. He had relatives there, and his son, John B. Floyd, who graduated from South Carolina College in 1829, had been a favorite pupil of Dr. Thomas Cooper. As already remarked, Floyd received the South Carolina electoral votes in the presidential contest of 1832.

[3] For Dew's interpretation of natural law see C. L. Becker, *The Declaration of Independence* (New York, 1922), p. 247; B. F. Wright, *American Interpretations of Natural Law* (Cambridge, Mass., 1931), p. 236. In the division headings Dew's irregular capitalization has been retained.

forced upon them," that Virginia especially could stand on this question "sans peur et sans reproche."

In Part II, *"Plans for the Abolition of Negro Slavery,"* Dew turned more directly to the debate, analyzing the proposals presented, refuting Randolph, Faulkner, and McDowell, endorsing Brown, Goode, and, for his subsequent stand, Leigh. He elaborated the impossibility of the legislative plans for emancipation and deportation, and the still greater absurdities of any proposals which might be made for emancipation without deportation. There should be no tampering with vested interests. "The great object of government," maintained Professor Dew, "is the protection of property. . . ." Like his forerunners in the debate, he was horrified at any proposal to request Federal aid. "Delusive prospect! Corrupting scheme!"

In developing Part III, *"Injustice and evils of Slavery,"* Dew again tested Bible arguments. Wavering a bit before the charge that slavery was opposed to the spirit of Christianity, he denied that either Old or New Testament commanded the removal of the institution, *once introduced.* The author approvingly cited the example of the Savior who "in no instance meddled with the established institutions of mankind. . . ." In assailing the Randolph plan and general antislavery contentions based on the natural rights theory, Dew had been making a flank attack on Jefferson; at this point in the discourse Jeffersonian ideas were subjected to frontal assault. Dew challenged Jefferson's assertions that slavery demoralized a people, and defended the virtues of a slaveholding society. He calmed his readers with words of safety and security, giving them an optimistic interpretation of the census figures, and a happy theory of the Negro's peaceful nature. Dew pointed a political moral by naming the protective tariff as the principal cause of the economic depression in the South. "It is not slave labor, then, which has produced our depression, but it is the action of the Federal Government which is ruining slave labor."

Certainly the booklet, termed by the late Professor William E. Dodd "the ablest of the works treating slavery from historical and social points of view," exerted an extraordinary influence on Southern thinking. Contemporary commentators avowed an almost uncanny conversion; later proslavery writers paid tribute to Dew's work. Less than a year after it was first published, Duff Green reprinted the essay in a six-cent edition under the expressed hope that it would rally the slaveholders against meddling Northern politicians. The *Review* had moved from the local to the national area of sectional conflict. John Quincy Adams, in an advantageous position for evaluating significant trends, believed that Dew's essay introduced a new era in American history.[4]

To clinch his argument against large-scale colonization, Dew had turned on the Liberian experiment and exposed the weaknesses and misfortunes of the modest repatriation enterprise sponsored by the American Colonization Society. This attack created a curious state of affairs, since the society was supported by many staunch conservatives. Jesse Burton Harrison, after corresponding with the officers of the American Colonization Society, wrote his antislavery *Review of the Slave Question* to counteract the influence which Dew's *Review* was enjoying in Virginia. Based largely on Marshall's speech in the House of Delegates, Harrison's materialistic essay was far from an endorsement of the radical emancipators in the debate. Under the initial handicap of addressing an audience more willing to be convinced by Dew, Harrison's effort also suffered by comparison with the persuasiveness and style of the earlier *Review*.[5]

The subsiding of antislavery expressions after the debate cannot be accredited simply to the arguments advanced by Dew and his kind. Their literature provided the language of justification, but the causes were deeper. Six factors contributed to the lapsing of the reform spirit once in evidence.

(1) It is obvious that the immediate occasion for the debate was the shattering of public confidence by the Southampton Insurrection. With the gradual restoration of composure the cry for preventive antislavery legislation faded.

(2) The Virginian's interest, fixed on the slavery problem only by force of a most dramatic occurrence, was soon dissipated over

[4] W. E. Dodd, *The Cotton Kingdom: A Chronicle of the Old South* (*The Chronicles of America*, Vol. XXVII, New Haven, 1919), pp. 49-53, 149; *Political Register*, II, 832 (Washington, Oct. 16, 1833); H. B. Adams, *Contributions to American Educational History*, I, 55. Dumas Malone in *The Public Life of Thomas Cooper: 1783-1839* (*Yale Historical Publications, Miscellany*, Vol. XVI, New Haven, 1926), p. 288, suggests that Dew was influenced by Cooper. On this question see W. S. Jenkins, *Pro-Slavery Thought in the Old South* (Chapel Hill, 1935), pp. 73-74, n. 68. Concerning the general importance of Dew see *ibid.*, p. 88. Eaton believes that Dodd has probably overemphasized the significance of Dew's work (*Freedom of Thought in the Old South*, p. 30, n. 95).

[5] "Slavery Question in Virginia," *American Quarterly Review*, XII, 379-426 (Dec., 1832); [J. B. Harrison,] *Review of the Slave Question* (Richmond, 1833); *Farmers Register*, I, 36 (June, 1833); Fox, *American Colonization Society*, pp. 10-11, 155; Fairfax and Francis Burton Harrison, *The Harrisons of Skimino* (privately printed, 1910), p. 102.

numerous events. The very day on which the slavery debate ended, January 25, 1832, John C. Calhoun by his deciding vote defeated in the Senate of the United States Van Buren's nomination as minister to Great Britain. News of this portentous development crowded accounts of the slavery debate in the Virginia journals. Less than ten days after this turn in national politics came John Marshall's impressive but futile attempt to protect the Cherokees in his famous decision, Worcester vs. Georgia. News from abroad, especially reports concerning the Reform Bill in England, absorbed the catholic-minded Southerner, who was prone to see in all foreign liberal movements a reflection of the American Revolution. After the diversions of the presidential election of 1832, the South was rocked by the nullification crisis.

From first to last the tariff controversy distracted Virginia liberals. It was indeed unfortunate for the reformers that the Virginia anti-slavery movement and the South Carolina tariff protest came at about the same historical moment, though the coincidence is in part explained by the fact that both were encouraged by the same condition, Southern economic depression. Floyd's message to the House of Delegates, as has already been remarked, not only called attention to the insurrection but entered into the problems of national politics and endorsed the South Carolina point of view. It is a well-known fact that Northern orators identified the institution of slavery with a low tariff policy. The Virginia debaters, in ascribing the economic deficiencies of the South to its labor system, played into the hands of Northern protectionists, who, much to the embarrassment of the legislators, hurled back their arguments at the Southern low tariff group. What slender chance remained for taking up the slavery question in the 1832-33 session of the Virginia legislature disappeared as the gathered clouds broke into the storm of nullification, exciting and divaricating Virginians. There was no mistaking the mood of legislators by January, 1833; they had enough major questions before them and sickened at the thought of another slavery debate.[6]

(3) Many people refrained from agitating the slave question for fear that it would threaten the unity of the state. Easterners declared they preferred to secede from western Virginia rather than repeat the 1832 tournament.

(4) A common explanation for the lack of antislavery expres-

[6] Concerning the mood in Richmond about the first of the year 1833 there are suggestive notes in the *Constitutional Whig*, Dec. 21, 1832, editorial; *Richmond Enquirer*, Feb. 12, 1833, Roane's remarks of Feb. 11, 1833.

sions after the debate is that the people, seeing nothing done despite the revolutionary discussion, accepted this inactivity as proof that the institution was irremovable. Lack of agreement as to method even among ardent antislavery spirits convinced observers that all ideas for emancipation and deportation were hopeless and, accordingly, that slavery had to be accepted and defended from its attackers.[7]

(5) To the riddle of antislavery decline, a popular answer is merely to state that when Southerners were making most progress Northern abolitionists meddled. The radicalism of Northern extremists undoubtedly did embarrass the milder reformers of Virginia, who did not relish the accusation of partnership with fanatics. This particular antislavery movement, however, seems to have been frustrated *before* Northern abolitionists were held responsible for Virginia's backsliding. It is significant that the leading proslavery argument of the time, Dew's *Review*, did not appear as a reaction against radical Yankees but in reply to the emancipators of Virginia herself.

(6) The most important reason for the ebb of the antislavery movement lies in the removal of a haunting fear that the whites of Virginia would soon be dangerously outnumbered by the blacks. Pessimists before and during the debate repeatedly and dolefully conjured up visions of many Santo Domingos and Southamptons to come. Delegates were alarmed at the appalling increase of Negroes as tallied in the census of 1830, an increase which promised to become still more grievous through the action of Cotton States' legislatures to check the small annual overflow of five thousand to eight thousand Virginia Negroes already going south.[8] But how different the actual event! Before the crucial year 1832 was out, the domestic slave trade enormously expanded, bringing with it a rise in the price of Negroes. The number of blacks exported to the far south from the upper slave states was never greater than in the 1832-36 period.[9]

[7] Ballagh, *A History of Slavery in Virginia*, p. 139; Munford, *Virginia's Attitude Toward Slavery and Secession*, p. 48; J. M. Batten, "Governor John Floyd," *John P. Branch Historical Papers of Randolph-Macon College*, Vol. IV, No. 1 (Ashland, Va., 1913), p. 39.

[8] For a significant reiteration of this point by a debater years after the event see the reminiscences of Summers as quoted in Mrs. S. C. P. Miller, "James McDowell," *Washington and Lee Historical Papers*, V (Baltimore, 1895), 99.

[9] W. H. Collins, *The Domestic Slave Trade of the Southern States* (New York, 1904), pp. 48-50. Frederic Bancroft in his *Slave-Trading in the Old South* (Baltimore, 1931), p. 385, remarks that 1835 and 1836 were peak years in the export of Virginia Negroes. Bancroft, figuring the Virginia exports on a basis of census population returns, calls the estimates made by Dew,

In place of being flooded with Negroes, Virginians were rid of their surplus blacks and had money in their pockets. Instead of the state's having to buy Negroes and send them to Africa, Mississippians and Louisianians paid cash and took them away.[10] Just as cotton planters were spurred to greater exertions by the rising quotations of their staple, so tobacco growers took on renewed hope with better prices for the leaf. Virginia shook off the depression only partly loosed since 1819 and entered on a new period of agricultural progress.[11]

With slavery now accepted as a permanent institution, defenders enlarged on the arguments advanced by the conservatives of the 1831-32 session and Dew in his *Review of the Debate*. The Virginia colleges played no mean part in this work of proclaiming slavery good in itself. Dew continued to expand his theories in the William and Mary classrooms and, four years after the publication of his *Review*, was made president of the college; William A. Smith, president of Randolph-Macon College, contributed *Lectures on the Philosophy and Practice of Slavery*; Albert T. Bledsoe, professor of mathematics at the University of Virginia, published his *Essay on Liberty and Slavery* to parry the abolitionist attack. They were supported in their basic argument by such Virginians as Thornton Stringfellow, author of *Slavery and Government* and *Slavery: Its Origin, Nature, and History*; George Fitzhugh, author of *Sociology for the*

Harrison, and the debaters, "surprizingly good guesses." For a Northern interpretation of the decline of 1832 antislavery sentiment, with emphasis on the increase in the slave trade and better prices of Negroes, see C. M. Weston, *Progress of Slavery in the United States* (Washington, 1857), pp. 199-201.

[10] From 1830 to 1840 the number of Negroes in eastern Virginia declined over 19,000. In 1840 within this same area the blacks outnumbered the whites by 68,000. The excess in 1830 had been 81,000. Note that the total population in eastern Virginia was 26,000 less in 1840 than in 1830.

Perhaps the shrewdest contemporary analysis of the factors which caused a decline of the 1831-32 antislavery movement is in a letter written from Virginia by a Northerner, July 29, 1835, printed in E. A. Andrews, *Slavery and the Domestic Slave Trade in the United States* (Boston, 1836), pp. 181-183. The writer of the letter was one of the agents sent out by the American Union for the Relief and Improvement of the Colored Race, a moderate antislavery society sponsored by Arthur Tappan (G. H. Barnes, *The Antislavery Impulse, 1830-1844*, New York, 1933, pp. 61-62, 224).

[11] Robert, *The Tobacco Kingdom: Plantation, Market, and Factory in Virginia and North Carolina, 1800-1860*, p. 143; A. O. Craven, *Soil Exhaustion as a Factor in the Agricultural History of Virginia and Maryland, 1606-1860* (Urbana, 1926), pp. 134-145. The first edition of Edmund Ruffin's epoch-making *Essay on Calcareous Manures*, the guidebook for agricultural revival in eastern Virginia, was published the very month of the slavery debate, Jan., 1832 (*ibid.*, p. 136, n. 52).

South, or the Failure of Free Society and *Cannibals All! or Slaves without Masters;* and the famous agriculturist, Edmund Ruffin, author of *The Political Economy of Slavery* and other essays.[12]

Not only sober philosophical treatise but colorful fiction registered the victory for conservatism. In the year 1832 John Pendleton Kennedy, a Marylander, published his *Swallow Barn* and set a powerful literary tradition by draping a romantic cloak over Virginia life and institutions. Four years later Nathaniel Beverley Tucker, son of St. George Tucker, friend and colleague of Thomas R. Dew, gave more positive defense of slavery in his polemic novel, *The Partisan Leader*. These works were guideposts on the road of fancy down which soon streamed countless caravans of patriarchal aristocrats and faithful retainers. Redolent with crape myrtle and honeysuckle, the paper pageants gave aid and comfort to defenders of the Southern way of life.[13]

Virginia was not without antislavery sentiment in the period from 1832 to 1860, but expressions of this nature were infrequent, cautious, and usually private.[14] The west continued more favorable to emancipation than did the east. Perhaps the most thorough public denunciation of slavery in Virginia during this era was that launched by Dr. Henry Ruffner, president of Washington College, in a speech printed in 1847 as *An Address to the People of West Virginia*.[15] The submerged current of antislavery conviction between the time of the slavery debate and the Emancipation Proclamation served to nurture the humanitarian feelings of Virginians. Some salved their consciences by continuing to support the American Colonization Society; others found opportunities for discreet service in the new campaign for religious instruction of the Negro.

Northern abolitionists soon adopted the Virginia speeches for several purposes, some of them contradictory: (1) They emphasized the more vulnerable remarks of the slavery men, such as Gholson's

[12] See espec. Jenkins, *Pro-Slavery Thought in the Old South*.

[13] J. B. Hubbell, *Virginia Life in Fiction* (Dallas, 1922), pp. 22-24; F. P. Gaines, *The Southern Plantation: A Study in the Development and the Accuracy of a Tradition* (New York, 1924), pp. 18-25; V. L. Parrington, *The Romantic Revolution in America, 1800-1860* (*Main Currents in American Thought*, II, New York, 1927), pp. 35-40, 46-56; *Dictionary of American Biography*, XIX, 36-37.

[14] See Eaton, *Freedom of Thought in the Old South*, espec. chap. x. On this problem Munford, *Virginia's Attitude Toward Slavery and Secession*, should be used with caution.

[15] Originally printed in Lexington, 1847. Reprinted in Wheeling, 1862; in Bridgewater, 1933.

assertion that the master had property in his slave's increase just as much as he had ownership in his mare's offspring.[16] (2) The abolitionists minimized the antislavery declarations as unsupported by public opinion and paraded the fact that the debate resulted in nothing constructive.[17] (3) Their favorite use of the debate was to quote as proof of their own arguments for abolition the antislavery statements made by Virginians in 1832; the purpose was to condemn the Southerners with the words of their own brethren.[18]

It was natural that Southerners seeking justification for slavery,

[16] W. L. Garrison, *Thoughts on African Colonization* (Boston, 1832), pp. 73-74; "Charter Oak," *The Legion of Liberty! and Force of Truth* (2d ed.; New York, 1843); Weston, *Progress of Slavery in the United States*, pp. 112-113.

[17] *Slavery and Emancipation* (Boston, 1834); Weston, *Progress of Slavery in the United States*, pp. 180-184. Weston gives all of chap. xiii to a perverted account of the debate.

[18] *The Liberator*, Vol. II, according to [Garrison,] *Garrison*, I, 251-252; Mrs. L. M. Child, *An Appeal in Favor of That Class of Americans Called Africans* (Boston, 1833), pp. 81-84; John Hersey, *An Appeal to Christians on the Subject of Slavery* (Baltimore, 1833), pp. 10-43 (Hersey's effort apparently was not to condemn the Southerners, but to prove that there was an energetic Southern antislavery sentiment); Mrs. L. M. Child, *The Evils of Slavery and the Cure of Slavery—The First Proved by the Opinion of Southerners Themselves—The Last Shown by Historical Evidence* (Newburyport, 1839), pp. 8-9; *The Legion of Liberty! and Force of Truth*; William Jay, *A Letter to the Right Rev. L. Silliman Ives* (3d ed.; n.p., 1848), pp. 5-6, reprinted in William Jay, *Miscellaneous Writings on Slavery* (Boston, 1853), pp. 457-458 (Randolph is called "T. M." instead of "T. J." and Thomas Marshall's 1832 remarks are dated 1845); D. R. Goodloe (North Carolinian), *The Southern Platform: or, Manual of Southern Sentiment on the Subject of Slavery* (Boston, 1858), pp. 42-54, section titled, "Debate on Emancipation in the Virginia Legislature in 1832"; H. R. Helper (North Carolinian), *The Impending Crisis of the South: How to Meet It*, pp. 203-204, 209-212, parts of chapter, "Southern Testimony Against Slavery"; *Address of the Hon. Edward Everett, Delivered in New York on the 4th of July, 1861*, pp. 31-32, quoted in George Livermore, *An Historical Research Respecting the Opinions of the Founders of the Republic on Negroes as Slaves, as Citizens, and as Soldiers* (Boston, 1862), pp. 15-18. For a development of the theme by a staunch abolitionist writing in the post-bellum period see Henry Wilson, *History of the Rise and Fall of the Slave Power in America* (3 vols.; Boston, 1872-77), I, chap. xiv. Quotations from the antislavery speeches, especially McDowell's, were freely used by Northern congressmen during the debates over the Wilmot Proviso and the Compromise of 1850. For quotations and the reply of McDowell, who was Representative from Virginia at the time, see *Appendix to the Congressional Globe*, 31st Congress, 1st Session, pp. 229, 1016, 1279, 1678. The interesting conversation concerning the debate, recorded in W. G. Hawkins, *Lunsford Lane, or Another Helper from North Carolina* (Boston, 1863), pp. 37-39, must be considered as apocryphal. See criticism of Hawkins in J. S. Bassett, *Anti-Slavery Leaders of North Carolina* (Johns Hopkins University, *Studies*, XVI, No. 6, Baltimore, 1898), p. 61.

though they borrowed and expanded the conservative reasoning of 1832, rarely made specific reference to the debate. The legislative controversy was too closely identified with denunciation of the Southern institution. Sometimes, as in the Reform Convention of 1851, the sectional spirit in Virginia prompted scoldings of the western district for its stand in 1832, but the subject was usually apologetically broached or passed over in silence.[19]

On February 20, 1860, Congressman Roger A. Pryor outlined in the House of Representatives the essential importance of the Virginia slavery debate from the slaveholders' point of view. In referring to that event he said:

Afterward, by common consent, the extravagances of a popular panic were covered with the vail of oblivion. But the effect of that interesting episode in the history of Virginia was not so evanescent and inconsequential. For the first time, citizens of a slaveholding community were driven, by the apparent insecurity of the system, to explore its foundations; and with a result for which very few persons were prepared. In contravention of traditional ideas, it was discovered and demonstrated that negro slavery, instead of being an accidental evil, which men tolerate merely for want of a practicable remedy, is an institution which exists in virtue of the most essential human interests, and the highest sanctions of the moral law. From that day, the slaveholder stood on surer and more solid ground. From that day, his conscience being clear, and his judgment convinced, he renounced the expedients of apology and extenuation, and planted himself on the impregnable basis of reason and right.[20]

It was an echo of John C. Calhoun, whose death in 1850 quieted the flesh, but not the ideas, of the restless South Carolinian.

The Jeffersonian critical spirit had passed away. Eighteenth-century conceptions of natural rights, free inquiry, and appeal to

---

[19] William O. Goode, *Speech of William O. Goode, Esq. . . . in the Virginia Reform Convention* (Richmond, 1851), p. 22; Rives, Speech of March 28, 1851 (*Supplement to Richmond Papers*, No. XV, photostatic copy, Virginia State Library); Slaughter, *Virginian History of African Colonization*, pp. 30, 55. According to Richard Hildreth, *Despotism in America* (Boston, 1840), pp. 94-95, a book written by a Virginia clergyman to aid the Colonization Society and made up of extracts from antislavery speeches in the Virginia House of Delegates (obviously the 1832 debate) "was denounced as *incendiary* by the Richmond Committee of Safety and by their order all the copies were delivered up and burnt in the public square."

[20] *The Congressional Globe*, 36th Congress, 1st Session, p. 844. It is significant that in this same fateful year, 1860, Charles H. Wynne, Richmond printer, published a new edition of J. T. Brown's speech.

reason were swept aside by a philosophy of defense, which combined literalism in religion with intolerance of social criticism. The South Carolina tide lapped on the sands of the Chesapeake. The Virginia slavery debate of 1832 had a consequential share in turning Southern thought into new channels.[21]

[21] For special essays on the shift in Southern thinking from Jeffersonianism to Calhounism see Dodd, *The Cotton Kingdom*, chap. iii; Parrington, *The Romantic Revolution in America, 1800-1860*, Bk. I; W. G. Bean, "Anti-Jeffersonianism in the Ante-Bellum South," *North Carolina Historical Review*, XII, 103-124 (April, 1935); Eaton, *Freedom of Thought in the Old South*, which the author suggests might well have the subtitle, "From Jefferson to Calhoun."

APPENDIX A

SELECTIONS FROM THE DEBATE

NOTE ON REPRINTING

With the exception of two minor speeches delivered before January 25, and several brief explanatory addresses made on that day, all of the debate proper, January 11-25, 1832, seems to have been printed early in the year 1832 in the *Richmond Enquirer*, in the *Constitutional Whig*, or in various pamphlets. The two unprinted speeches made in the debate before the final day were those by Halyburton on January 23, and by Jones on January 24. Brief notices of these speeches appeared at the time they were made. On January 25, the day of the final voting, there were eleven speeches, usually short explanations of the votes about to be cast. The speakers were Rutherfoord, Bolling, Patteson of Buckingham, Booker, Brodnax, Jones, Ball, Gallaher, Roane, Gholson, and Moore, in the order named. Of these speeches only four were printed: Bolling's speech, apparently the major oration of the day, and the remarks of Patteson, Ball, and Gallaher.

Although both *Richmond Enquirer* and *Constitutional Whig* agree on the dating and order of the speeches in their summaries of proceedings immediately after each day's debate in the House of Delegates, the full accounts of the speeches, usually published weeks later, are sometimes erroneously dated. Eight speeches, when reported in full by the *Enquirer*, are given false dates: the two made on January 12, Gholson and Rives; the two made on January 13, Brodnax and Bruce; the four made on January 14, Powell, Daniel, Faulkner, and Marshall. Since the speeches by Brodnax, Faulkner, and Marshall were each reprinted in 1832 in pamphlet form from the *Enquirer*, these three pamphlets carry the erroneous dates. The second edition of the Marshall pamphlet is correctly dated. A fourth pamphlet, the Randolph pamphlet, is incorrectly dated, but, as noted below, not from the same cause as the others.

It is not difficult to trace the history of the misdating of the speeches made January 12, 13, and 14. The *Enquirer*, eight days after the beginning of the debate, began reporting the speeches in full. In that issue, January 19, 1832, the *Enquirer* gave the proper date, "*Wednesday, January* 11," for the proceedings of the first day and presented detailed accounts of the speeches made at that time.

In the next issue, January 21, 1832, the account of the debate was continued under the heading, "[SECOND DAY.]—*Wednesday, January* 18" when it should have been "Thursday, January 12." Likewise the *Enquirer* of January 24, 26, and 28 erroneously headed the speeches of Friday, January 13, as "[THIRD DAY.]—*Thursday, January* 19." And the *Enquirer* of January 31 and February 2 titled the speeches of Saturday, January 14 as "[FOURTH DAY]—*Friday, January* 20." On February 4, however, the *Enquirer* recovered the correct dating of the speeches, which it was reprinting, by giving the heading, "[FIFTH DAY]—*Monday, January* 16."

The second Randolph speech, that made Friday, January 20, appeared in detailed form in the *Whig*, February 11, but not in the *Enquirer*. In the *Whig* the speech was undated. In the pamphlet edition, by some accident, the date is erroneously printed as Saturday, January 21. The only suggestion as to the origin of this error which presents itself is that the pamphlet printer became confused because the first brief accounts of the speech appeared in January 21 editions of both *Whig* and *Enquirer*.

As suggested above, the sequence and dates of the speeches used in this book are taken from the brief summaries in the *Enquirer* and *Whig* immediately after the days' sessions. The speeches of the first day, Wednesday, January 11, are listed in the *Enquirer*, January 12, and the *Whig*, January 13; those of the second day, in the *Enquirer*, January 14, and the *Whig*, January 17; those of the third day, in the *Enquirer*, January 14, and the *Whig*, January 17; those of the fourth day, in the *Enquirer*, January 17, and the *Whig*, January 17; those of the fifth day, Monday, January 16, in the *Enquirer*, January 17, and the *Whig*, January 17; those of the sixth day, in the *Enquirer*, January 19, and the *Whig*, January 19; those of the seventh day, in the *Enquirer*, January 19, and the *Whig*, January 19; those of the eighth day, in the *Enquirer*, January 21, and the *Whig*, January 21; those of the ninth day, in the *Enquirer*, January 21, and the *Whig*, January 21; that of the tenth day, in the *Enquirer*, January 24, and the *Whig*, January 24; those of the eleventh day, Monday, January 23, in the *Enquirer*, January 24, and the *Whig*, January 24; those of the twelfth day, in the *Enquirer*, January 26, and the *Whig*, January 26; those of the thirteenth day, in the *Enquirer*, January 26 (with correction of January 28), and the *Whig*, January 28.

In printing extracts from the speeches the intention has been to preserve intact the 1832 texts, typographical errors in the original sources excepted. Although old style spelling and punctuation have been retained, it has been assumed that the printer was responsible for such variants as "developement," "absoluteism," "etherial," and the like. Accordingly, words of this type have been corrected.

For most of the debate there are sources other than the ones used and cited in preparing the selections below. The discourses of the following speakers may be found in the additional sources indicated. First day: Goode (the report only a "meagre outline"), *Whig*, January 17; Bryce, *Whig*, January 19; Moore, *Whig*, January 17; Bolling, *Enquirer*, January 19, and *Whig*, January 19; Randolph, *Whig*, January 19. Second day: Gholson, *Whig*, January 21, 26; Rives, *Whig*, January 19. Third day: Brodnax, *Enquirer*, January 24, 28, and *Whig*, February 2, 4, 7; Bruce, *Whig*, January 19. Fourth day: Powell, *Whig*, January 21; Daniel, *Whig*, January 26; Faulkner, *Enquirer*, January 31, February 2, and *Whig*, January 24; Marshall, *Enquirer*, February 2, *Whig*, January 24, and the first edition of the pamphlet, *The Speech of Thomas Marshall, in the House of Delegates of Virginia, on the Abolition of Slavery, Delivered Friday, January 20, 1832* (Richmond, 1832), erroneously dated as noted above. Fifth day: Roane, *Whig*, January 24; Wood, *Whig*, January 26; Preston, *Whig*, January 28. Sixth day: Summers, *Whig*, January 31; Chandler, *Enquirer*, February 24, and *Whig*, January 28. Seventh day: Brown, *Enquirer*, March 6, 8, 10, *Whig*, February 9, and the pamphlet published in 1860 by Chas. H. Wynne, of Richmond, "Re-printed from Pamphlet copy of 1832"; Garland, *Whig*, February 2. Eighth day: none. Ninth day: Randolph, *Whig*, February 11; Berry, *Whig*, February 14. Tenth day: M'Dowell, *Whig*, March 26. Eleventh day: none. Twelfth day: none. Thirteenth day: Bolling, *Enquirer*, March 30; Patteson, *Whig*, March 28. Apparently the texts are the same in the various sources

PLAN OF THE DEBATE

1832
January

11	FIRST DAY WEDNESDAY	(A)	Wm. O. Goode, Mecklenburg County
		(B)	Jas. G. Bryce, Frederick County
		(C)	Sam. M'D. Moore, Rockbridge County
		(D)	Philip A. Bolling, Buckingham County
		(E)	Thomas J. Randolph, Albemarle County

12	SECOND DAY THURSDAY	(A) Jas. H. Gholson, Brunswick County
		(B) Wm. M. Rives, Campbell County
13	THIRD DAY FRIDAY	(A) Wm. H. Brodnax, Dinwiddie County
		(B) Jas. C. Bruce, Halifax County
14	FOURTH DAY SATURDAY	(A) Rob't. D. Powell, Spottsylvania County
		(B) Wm. Daniel, Jr., Campbell County
		(C) Charles J. Faulkner, Berkeley County
		(D) Thos. Marshall, Fauquier County
16	FIFTH DAY MONDAY	(A) Wm. H. Roane, Hanover County
		(B) Rice W. Wood, Albemarle County
		(C) Wm. B. Preston, Montgomery County
17	SIXTH DAY TUESDAY	(A) Alex. G. Knox, Mecklenburg County
		(B) Geo. W. Summers, Kanawha County
		(C) John A. Chandler, Norfolk County
18	SEVENTH DAY WEDNESDAY	(A) John T. Brown, Town of Petersburg
		(B) Samuel M. Garland, Amherst County
19	EIGHTH DAY THURSDAY	(A) George I. Williams, Harrison County
		(B) John E. Shell, Brunswick County
20	NINTH DAY FRIDAY	(A) Thomas J. Randolph, Albemarle County
		(B) Willoughby Newton, Westmoreland County
		(C) Henry Berry, Jefferson County
21	TENTH DAY SATURDAY	(A) Jas. M'Dowell, Jr., Rockbridge County
23	ELEVENTH DAY MONDAY	(A) John C. Campbell, Brooke County

24	TWELFTH DAY TUESDAY	(A) Wm. O. Goode, Mecklenburg County (B) Sam. M'D. Moore, Rockbridge County
25	THIRTEENTH DAY WEDNESDAY	(A) Philip A. Bolling, Buckingham County (B) Wm. N. Patteson, Buckingham County (C) Spencer M. Ball, Fairfax County (D) John S. Gallaher, Jefferson County

FIRST DAY, WEDNESDAY, JANUARY 11, 1832

(For parliamentary movements on January 11 see pp. 18-19.)

(A) WM. O. GOODE, Mecklenburg County

[*Richmond Enquirer*, Jan. 19, 1832.] Mr. GOODE said . . . But he now found that it had become his imperious duty, since no other individual seemed disposed to assume the task—to step forward, in order, if possible, to arrest a misguided and pernicious course of legislation, by moving that the Committee on the subject of Slaves and Free Negroes, should be discharged from the consideration of the question of emancipation, because he believed that the Legislature of Virginia was now considering whether they would confiscate the property of the citizens—a question which it had no right to act upon or consider.—The consideration of this subject had given rise to the diffusion of opinions highly injurious. It was well known that the public press had embarked in the discussion of the subject, and in favor of abolition: and he need not speak of the power of the press, which was universally acknowledged. These expressions of opinion had produced, and were producing, the most disastrous effects,—it being impossible to touch this subject, without impairing the value of the property of the Slave-holders. . . .

(B) JAS. G. BRYCE, Frederick County

[*Richmond Enquirer*, Jan. 19, 1832.] Mr. BRYCE of F., said . . . He had risen to state that he represented a chivalrous and generous people, who went the whole length with their Eastern brethren; and he should oppose all schemes of emancipation, considering himself instructed by the general sense of his constituents to take that course. But he hoped the Committee would be allowed to report on the petitions which were from various parts of the country, in order that the views of the Committee might be spread abroad among the people, that they might decide.

(C) SAM. M'D. MOORE, Rockbridge County

[*Richmond Enquirer*, Jan. 19, 1832.] Mr. MOORE rose and said . . .

. . . But, Sir, I must proceed to point out some of the most prominent evils arising from the existence of slavery among us. And among these, the first I shall mention, is the irresistible tendency which it has, to undermine and destroy every thing like virtue and morality in the community. I think I may safely assert, that ignorance is the inseparable companion of slavery, and that the desire of freedom is the inevitable consequence of implanting in the human mind any useful degree of intelligence; it is therefore the policy of the master, that the ignorance of his slaves shall be as profound as possible. And such a state of ignorance is wholly incompatible with the existence of any moral exalted feeling in the breast of the slave. It renders him incapable of deciding between right and wrong, of judging of the enormity of crime, or of estimating the high satisfaction which the performance of an honorable act affords to more intelligent beings. He is never actuated by those noble and inspiring motives which prompt the free to the performance of creditable and praiseworthy deeds; on the contrary his early habits, pursuits and associations, are such as to bring into action all his most vicious propensities. He is habituated from his infancy to sacrifice truth, without remorse, as the only means of escaping punishment, which is too apt to be inflicted, whether merited or not. The candid avowal of a fault, which a kind parent is disposed to regard in his child as the evidence of merit, is sure to be considered by the master as insolence in a slave, and to furnish additional reason for inflicting punishment upon him. The slave perceives that he can never attain to the least distinction in society, however fair and unexceptionable his conduct may be, or even to an equality with the lowest class of free men; and that, however innocent he may be, he is often liable to the severest punishment, at the will of hireling overseers, without even the form of a trial. . . . He looks upon the whole white population as participating in the wrongs he endures, and never scruples to revenge himself by injuring their property; and he is never deterred from the commission of theft, except by fear of the punishment consequent on detection. The demoralizing influence of the indiscriminate intercourse of the sexes among our slave population, need only to be hinted at, to be fully understood. Can it be expected, Sir, or will it be contended, that where so large a mass of the population of the country is corrupt, that the other classes can entirely escape the contagion? Sir, it is impossible! and the dissolute habits of a large number of our citizens, especially of the very poorest class is too notorious to be denied, and the cause of it is too obvious to be disputed. Far be it from me, Mr. Speaker, to assert, that virtue and morality cannot at all exist among the free, where slavery is allowed, or that there are not many high-minded, honorable, virtuous and patriotic individuals even in those parts of the State, where the slaves are most numerous. I know there are many such. I only contend, that it is impossible in the nature of things, that slaves can be virtuous and moral, and that their vices must have to some extent, an injudicious influence upon the morals of the free.

There is another, and perhaps a less questionable evil, growing out of the existence of slavery in this country, which cannot have escaped the observation, or failed to have elicited the profound regrets of every patriotic and reflecting individual in the Assembly. I allude, Sir, to the prevalent, and almost universal indisposition of the free population, to engage in the cultivation of the soil—that species of labor, upon which the prosperity of every country chiefly depends. That being the species of labor in which slaves are usually employed, it is very generally regarded as a mark of servitude, and consequently as degrading and disreputable. . . . How many young men, (who were it not for the prevailing prejudices of the country, might gain an honorable and honest subsistence by cultivating the soil,) do we see, attempting to force themselves into professions already crowded to excess, in order to obtain a precarious subsistence? and how many of these do we see resort to intemperance to drown reflection, when want of success has driven them to despair? . . .

A third consequence of slavery is, that it detracts from the ability of a country to defend itself against foreign aggression. . . .

. . . The market for slaves may be considered then, as closed forever, and the inevitable consequence will be, that the blacks will continue to increase without any check whatsoever; the slave-holders will be compelled in order to find them employment to drive off their poor white tenants from their lands; the small slave-holders will be compelled to sell out and remove, until in the course of some twenty or thirty years, the disproportion between the blacks and whites, will become so great, that the slaves will attempt to recover their liberty; and then the consequences which I have predicted, and which is so much to be deprecated, will inevitably ensue.

I have so far, Mr. Speaker, confined my attention to the injurious and dangerous consequences of slavery as they affect the white population exclusively: I must now take a short view of slavery as it affects the slaves themselves. "That all men are by nature free and equal" is a truth held sacred by every American, and by every Republican, throughout the world. And I presume it cannot be denied in this Hall, as a general principle, that it is an act of injustice, tyranny, and oppression, to hold any part of the human race in bondage against their consent. That circumstances may exist which put it out of the power of the owners for a time to grant their slaves liberty, I admit to be possible; and if they do exist in any case, it may excuse, but not justify, the owner in holding them. The right to the enjoyment of liberty, is one of those perfect, inherent and inalienable rights, which pertain to the whole human race, and of which they can never be divested, except by an act of gross injustice. I may be told, Sir, as an argument in favor of retaining our slaves, that their condition is preferable to that of the laboring class of people in Europe. And, Sir, it will afford me the most heart-felt satisfaction to declare my belief, that such is the fact; at all events, it is certain that slavery exists in a milder form than it has done in any other portion of the world.—But at the same time it must be remembered, that slavery is at best, but an intolerable evil, and can never be submitted to, except from stern necessity. It must also be confessed, that although the treatment of our slaves is in the general as mild and humane as it can be, that it must always happen, that there will be found hundreds of individuals, who, owing either to the natural ferocity of their dispositions, or to the effects of intemperance, will be guilty of cruelty and barbarity towards their slaves, which is almost intolerable, and at which humanity revolts. But even if slavery was not injurious to ourselves, and the condition of the slave was ten times as happy as it is, it is enough for us to know, that we have no right to hold them against their consent, to induce us to make a vigorous effort to send them from among us. Liberty is too dear to the heart of man, ever to be given up for any earthly consideration. . . .

(D) PHILIP A. BOLLING, Buckingham County

[*The Speeches of Philip A. Bolling, (of Buckingham,) in the House of Delegates of Virginia, on the Policy of the State in Relation to Her Colored Population: Delivered on the 11th and 25th of January, 1832*, 2d ed., Richmond, 1832, p. 2.] MR. BOLLING rose and addressed the house. . . .

[p. 4] There is yet another evil growing out of our present system of slavery. It drives from us the laboring man—the honest, industrious poor. . . . The small freeholders are driven off also. . . . The hard struggle they have to make for the bare necessities of life— to say nothing of its luxuries—puts an effectual extinguisher upon all the humble aspirations of their ambition. The sparseness of the white population, opposes almost an insurmountable obstacle in the way of the education of their children. . . .

[p. 5] So exhausted is our soil, so depressed our markets, and so dear is slave labor, that it is as much as the master can do to clothe and feed his slaves—nay, sir, often more than he can do; for, if you will go into the credit stores and pop-shops, (with which the whole country is thronged) you will find that, with very few exceptions, the slave-holder has there become very deeply entangled—the embarrassment mainly incurred to clothe and feed his slaves. The slave is clothed and fed, that he may labor for victuals and clothes—a beautiful operation!—Thus, sir, the master of the slave absolutely belongs to the merchant, and has to labor—and labor hard—for their benefit. He is literally their bondsman. Finally, when they have extracted from him all they can, his account is put into the lawyer's hand for collection, and he has to raise the money or go to jail. Then steps forward the paper-shaver, (another fungus of our present condition) and kindly proffers the money at *thirty-three and a third* per cent. Thus the poor devil of a master is finally stripped of all he has, to swell the importance of these gentry. . . .

(E) THOMAS J. RANDOLPH, Albemarle County

[*Richmond Enquirer,* Jan. 19, 1832.] Mr. RANDOLPH rose and said:

. . . The amendment I had the honor to offer was not intended as a fire-brand thrown into this House; but designed to put the subject quietly off from our consideration to that of the people. I am not prepared to vote definitively upon any proposition that is not to be submitted to the people. When they have expressed their wishes at the polls, then can we act advisedly, but not till then. . . .

Gentlemen charge upon the discussion of this subject the excitements of the public mind. . . . No, Sir; it is the unfortunate occurrences of the last six months, which has awakened the public mind to the grave circumstances of our condition; it is the dark, the appalling, the despairing future. If exportation ceases, the slave population, at its hitherto ratio of increase, must, in 1860, be 1,028,000; in 1900, 2,910,000. Is it wise to fold our arms in indifference upon it, as an irremediable evil? . . . The hour of eradication of the evil is advancing—it must come.—Whether it is effected by the energy of our own minds, or by the bloody scenes of Southampton and St. Domingo, is a tale for future history!

SECOND DAY, THURSDAY, JANUARY 12, 1832

(A) JAS. H. GHOLSON, Brunswick County

[*Richmond Enquirer,* Jan. 21, 1832.] Mr. GHOLSON rose and said . . .

It has always (perhaps erroneously) been considered by that steady and old-fashioned people [of Brunswick County], that the owner of land had a reasonable right to its annual profits; the owner of orchards, to their annual fruits; the owner of brood mares, to their product; and the owner of female slaves, to their *increase*. We have not the fine-spun intelligence, nor legal acumen, to discover the technical distinctions drawn by gentlemen. The legal maxim of *"Partus sequitur ventrem"* is coeval with the existence of the right of property itself, and is founded in wisdom and justice. It is on the justice and inviolability of this maxim, that the master foregoes the service of the female slave; has her nursed and attended during the period of her gestation, and raises the helpless and infant offspring. The value of the property justifies the expense; and I do not hesitate to say, that in its increase consists much of our wealth. . . .

But, Sir, another and a still stranger light has broken in upon us. The gentleman from Rockbridge, (Mr. Moore,) disdaining to examine this subject *under* the Constitution and laws, has ascended to the very fountain of our political power, and rests himself upon our bill of rights. "All men, by nature, are equally free and independent." The gentleman thinks that here he has found a power sufficiently comprehensive and resistless to burst asunder the chains of slavery, and set the captive free. . . . But the gentleman's construction of the Bill of Rights is not just. The section to which he has referred is only a declaration of the *natural* rights of man—not a declaration of the powers of this Government, or of social obligations or rights of *society*. If the gentleman's construction should obtain, the bands which bind society together would at once dissolve—the relations of husband and wife, parent and child, master and apprentice, master and servant, governor and governed, would end, and even our present deliberations would be "most strange and unnatural."

. . . Show me, sir that the salvation or existence of this society depends on the adoption of this substitute, and with submission, I will cry *"Salus populi Suprema est Lex."* Show me that the horrors of insurrection are gathering round us, and this is our only refuge, and promptly will I exclaim *"inter arma silent leges."* Pardon me, however, if, on a subject of this high import, I reject the evidences offered here. . . . No, Sir; the people of our country again sleep quietly on their pillows, and would, in all probability, have enjoyed uninterrupted repose, had it not been for this false legislative cry of "Wolf!" "Wolf!" . . .

. . . Sir, I have too much respect for certain Northern Governments within this Union, to believe, that they will, upon reflection, tolerate any longer, the publication and circulation of the dangerous and incendiary productions, which have of late issued from their press. If, however, in this I am disappointed; and if, from the peculiar organization of the Governments under which we live, there is no mode of peaceable redress secured to us, I declare, on the responsibility of the public station I now occupy, that rather than submit to the continuance of evils like these, without the hope of redress, I would appeal to *war*, and deem it the lesser evil. . . .

We are not responsible for the existence of slavery amongst us. It is here; and no reproaches on the one hand, or regrets on the other, can avoid it. But it is the duty of a just, wise and virtuous people, to mitigate its evils to the utmost extent of their ability, and to make it subservient to the best purposes of society; and on this ground I challenge investigation. I will not discuss the abstract question of the right of slavery: but I will say that the slaves of Va. are as happy a laboring class as exists upon the habitable globe. They are as well fed, as well clothed, and as well treated. In health, but reasonable labour is required of them—in sickness, they are nursed and attended to. In times of plenty, they live in waste—in times of scarcity, they do not want—they are content to-day, and have no care or anxiety for to-morrow. Cruel treatment of them is discountenanced by society, and until of late, their privileges were daily extending. Among what labouring class will you find more happiness and less misery? Not among the serfs and labouring poor of Europe! No, Sir.—Nor among the servants to the North of us.

Our slave population is not only a happy one, but it is a contented, peaceful and harmless one. . . . Sir, during all this time [the last sixty years], we have had *one insurrection*. . . .

Mr. Speaker, gentlemen who draw these gloomy pictures of Eastern wealth and agriculture, are—my life upon it!—better poets than planters. . . . We cannot judge the general character of cultivation in a country, by that which surrounds its cities, or borders its navigable streams. We must visit the interior—and if gentlemen will do this, they will find to their astonishment, that Virginia does not fear comparison as much as they had supposed. They will find, Sir, that excepting Pennsylvania, she might compare without disparagement, with any other State in the Union. . . .

Although this attempt to prove Virginia exhausted and impoverished, suits neither my taste nor my opinions, I might perhaps have been content, had gentlemen paused here. Poverty, though a heavy misfortune, is no crime: But the gentleman from Buckingham, in his ardent zeal to attribute the "whole sum of human ills" to this self-same cause of slavery, has informed us, that our *intelligence, our morality, our character,* our reputation for *chivalry* and *honor* are impaired and declining.... I indulge a faint hope that the gentleman is mistaken; his *poetic* mind, on the present occasion, is tinged you know, Mr. Speaker, with a gloomy cast.—But, then, his station and opportunities enable him to know.... As to our national character, I trust it vindicates itself, and requires no defence at my hands. I discover nothing in the annals of the past, or in the history of the current times, to impair its dignity, or sully its purity....

[*Richmond Enquirer*, Jan. 24, 1832.] ... If we effect during our present deliberations, the object which seems to meet the approbation of all, we will in my judgment have done enough; and put into requisition as much of the means and energy of the State, as is reasonable for the present.—I allude to the removal of the *free* colored population, Sir.... The free blacks comprise nearly one-tenth of the entire black population of the State; it is the most depraved, dissolute, miserable and dangerous portion of it—operates as the connecting link between the class of abandoned and irreclaimable whites, and the slaves themselves.—With no regular occupations to restrain them from mischief, they act as the procurers of news, and the carriers of intelligence; and by their presence and association, are continually reminding the slave, of the difference in their *condition*, and the bondage in which *he* lives....

... Sir, we are in debt; and professing to be an honest people, we are anxious to pay. Our slaves constitute the largest portion of our wealth, and by their value, regulate the price of nearly all the property we possess. Their value on the other hand, is regulated by the demand for it in the western markets; and any measures which should close those markets against us, would essentially impair our wealth and prosperity.... That the adoption of this scheme, will result in the closure of every market in the Union against this property, will not, I presume, be controverted....

The gentleman from Albemarle has informed us, that thousands of families are anxiously awaiting the decision of this question. I agree with him, Sir; but I differ with him as to the feelings and sentiments which create their solicitude.... If you say that slaves shall not be private property within your jurisdiction, you force from you every individual whose removal will enable him to avoid the operation of your law, and to enjoy, unmolested, the property which he feels to be his own....

(B) WM. M. RIVES, Campbell County

[*Richmond Enquirer*, Jan. 21, 1832.] Mr. RIVES said ... The plan indicated in the substitute, by which to accomplish the great object of diminishing and ultimately getting rid of the evils of slavery, appeared to be so plain and simple that all might understand it—it was altogether prospective in its operation, and was "solidly practical." . . .

. . . He would not use the word defy, but he would invite any gentleman, however talented, to point out a mode of resuscitating the declining fortunes of lower Virginia, so sure and efficient (removal of the evils of slavery excepted) as a judicious system of internal improvement, that should draw the produce of Middle and Western Virginia to the market towns of the East. . . . Yet the large slave-holders of the lower country, continually opposed all measures calculated to accomplish these purposes. And it seemed to him, that this strange course could not be accounted for otherwise, than by the supposition that, desirous of perpetuating the evils of slavery, they apprehended that this object would be defeated, by the establishment of large commercial emporiums among us: that the activity, enterprise and intelligence generated by, and inseparably attendant on, extended and prosperous trade; and the prosperity, activity and enterprise thereby diffused over the surrounding country, would introduce a spirit and intelligence fatal to the hope of perpetuating slavery.

Again; the large slave-holders had the means of educating their sons, at any college or university they pleased; and many of them wisely discharged their parental duty in this respect. But let any plan be proposed, by which to facilitate and improve the education of the middle and poor classes of society, it met with the decided opposition of the large slave-holder; although the plan may have succeeded admirably in other States, and be highly recommended in this. . . . Adding to the intelligence, morality and christianity of the poor part of the community, might not be favorable to the perpetuation of slavery.

The right of suffrage might be liberally extended in other States, but its extension had been warmly opposed and curtailed here: it might be safe and proper in free States, but it met with opposition here, on account of the existence of slavery? Other instances might be adduced to illustrate the strange and anti-patriotic sentiment generated by the evil of slavery; but he would forbear. He had spoken of large slave-holders; he knew there were bright exceptions among them; he knew also, that the remarks did not apply to small slave-holders, many of whom were willing to give up their slaves, if means could be provided of sending them off; at least, this was the case in Campbell. . . .

THIRD DAY, FRIDAY, JANUARY 13, 1832

(A) WM. H. BRODNAX, Dinwiddie County

[*The Speech of William H. Brodnax, (of Dinwiddie) in the House of Delegates of Virginia, on the Policy of the State with Respect to its Colored Population. Delivered January 19* [sic], *1832, Richmond, 1832, p. 3.*] MR. BRODNAX rose and addressed the house. . . .

[p. 8] Sir, I confidently believe that *a plan* can be devised to mitigate, if not subdue, the evil which presses so sorely upon us, entirely consistent with the principles which have been so ably and so gallantly maintained by gentlemen from my own region of country, where those principles have ever been regarded as sacred and inviolable; and yet comprehending all that our brethren from other divisions of the state, and holding other opinions, ought to desire. . . .

[p. 10] That *slavery in Virginia is an evil*, and a transcendent evil, it would be idle, and more than idle, for any human being to doubt or deny. It is a mildew which has blighted in its course every region it has touched, from the creation of the world. . . .

[p. 11] The people, sir, have long deeply felt the embarrassment and importance of the subject—and, stimulated by recent occurrences, they have lately, with a simultaneous movement and united voice, demanded our interposition, and required that *"something"* should be done. . . .

[p. 12] Any scheme for the gradual diminution, or ultimate extermination of the black population of Virginia, should be based, as a substratum, on certain great cardinal principles of justice, morality, and political expediency, about which I had hoped but little diversity of opinion would be found to exist. . . .

1st. That no emancipation of slaves should ever be tolerated, unaccompanied by their immediate removal from among us.

2d. That no system should be introduced, which is calculated to interfere with, or weaken the *security* of private property, or affect its *value*.—And

3d. That not a single slave, or any other property he possesses, should be taken from its owner, *without his own consent*, or an ample compensation for its value.

. . . Much may be done if not to remove this evil, at least to abate its extent—to limit its effects—and to take from it, its most dangerous and most fearful tendencies. . . .

[p. 18] But, Mr. Speaker, has not another objection to this [Randolph] plan occurred to you, of still more delicate and insuperable character? Suppose it submitted;—to whom will you submit it?

Will you submit it to those who own the property, or to those who do not? . . .

[p. 21] Mr. Speaker, in the course of this discussion many things have been said on both sides, the expression of which I sincerely regretted. . . . I know, sir, that the gentleman from Rockbridge is one of the last who would willingly stand as an ally by the side of such incendiaries as Garrison and Walker—and yet he has used the very idea, and nearly in the very words, which is so conspicuously emblazoned to our slaves by those execrable pamphleteers. . . .

[p. 22] I heard also, Mr. Speaker, with regret, unfavorable opinions of our brethren of other states, expressed perhaps with too much force, and denunciations indulged in entirely too general, against the "yankees;" for instance, in consequence of the shameless conduct of some few miscreants among them, who have endeavored, by incendiary publications, to excite our slaves to insurrection. Shall we talk of war with our sister states, because a Garrison or a Walker may disgrace their soil? . . . [p. 23] Our northern brethren no longer, as was the case some years ago, look on every Virginia slave-holder, as identified with a negro driver in the Mauritius, who forces them to labor night and day, with scarcely an intermission, and keeps them up with a cart whip: that they are fed on cotton-seed, or for the slightest offence cruelly bastinandoed, while confined naked on their backs, with their eyes exposed to a scorching sun, as the Romans formerly punished their desperate culprits. They have found out, that all these are mistakes; and that public sentiment in Virginia, will not tolerate the cruel or improper treatment of slaves: that in point of fact, their condition is superior to that of the peasantry of any other country, in possessing the ordinary comforts of life. I regard them myself, as exempt from many of the evils incident to laboring classes in other countries—They are well fed and well clothed—Famine, which reaches others, is never allowed, even from policy, to affect them. They have no care on their minds to provide a subsistence, and are, when they have good masters, I believe in a happy condition. And in this light is the subject now generally regarded by strangers of intelligence, who never condescend to take their opinions from the miserable effusions of such editors as have been alluded to. A great many of our prejudices against them, on the other hand, have been discovered to be unfounded. We have learnt that it is not fair to judge of a whole people from the specimens exhibited of travelling pedlars, or needy adventurers. And I am happy in expressing it as my opinion, that a better state of feeling between us is growing up continually, and that it ought to be cherished. . . .

[p. 29] There are no fair principles of calculation which can be applied to our previous history, or to the actual returns of our census, whether including short or more extending periods of time, which will not, I think, indicate a ratio of increase, of the whole African race in Virginia, of less than 6,000 a year. By a removal then of 6,000 annually from the territory of Virginia, the capital stock would at the least be kept stationary, if not reduced—while our white population would be increasing at an accelerated pace. . . .

[p. 32] And will the expense involved—$200,000—be considered as presenting an insuperable obstacle? . . . $200,000 on the great state of Virginia, is less than 30 cents a head on her white inhabitants. And who would refuse to pay that? Abstinence from two or three glasses of toddy at the court house, would pay it in one day. What addition would it make to our present burdens? . . . The proposed amount, would only increase the burden 20 per cent. . . .

I have supposed it not only probable, but approaching certainty, [p. 33] that we might obtain considerable resources from the federal government, to which we are *entitled*, on every consideration of equal justice, and which we might consistently receive, without the slightest violation of those strict state right principles which distinguish our Virginia political school, and of which I profess myself a disciple. Of the public lands held by the general government, a large portion, it will be recollected, was ceded by Virginia—a portion too, which was exceedingly valuable. . . .

[p. 34] For the transportation of our free negroes alone, I have endeavored to shew our state resources are amply sufficient. Let us, then, commence in effecting that, about which most of us are agreed —and which is all that could, for the present, be effected, whatever may be the ulterior object of any—the removal of the free persons of color. When this shall have been completed—if in its process it shall have demonstrated the practicability of this plan of gradual deportation—and if the means shall by that time be within our control with which to effect it, as I hope I have shewn was at least probable, what is to prevent our going on with the system, by the removal, annually, of as many as 6,000 of those who are now slaves? We shall have the means, I trust, of purchasing this number at fair prices. But, it is my decided belief, that this will not become necessary—or, at any rate, beyond a limited extent. . . .

(B) JAS. C. BRUCE, Halifax County

[*Richmond Enquirer*, Jan. 26, 1832.] Mr. BRUCE said . . . I beg gentlemen to recollect, that I do not stand here as an advocate for slavery. I see, and feel too, the evils of the system. I justify it on the grounds of necessity. It is here that all the wise and the good of our land who have gone before us, have rested it; and here too it will continue to rest. The substitute which has been offered, is said to be the offspring of the mind of the immortal Jefferson—one of the wisest patriots and most profound thinkers which our country has ever produced. Its glaring and palpable defects serve to show us the difficulty, or rather the impossibility, of devising any scheme of emancipation which shall be practicable, and not at the same time in direct violation of the rights of property. . . .

FOURTH DAY, SATURDAY, JANUARY 14, 1832

(A) ROB'T. D. POWELL, Spottsylvania County

[*Richmond Enquirer*, Jan. 31, 1832.] Mr. POWELL rose and said . . .

Mr. Speaker; I do not deem this an appropriate occasion to discuss the abstract question of slavery; although certainly the very fundamental principles upon which our free institutions so highly prized and so justly boasted of, are based, ALL go to repudiate it. . . . I can scarcely persuade myself that there is a solitary gentleman in this house who will not readily admit that slavery is an evil, and that its removal, if practicable, would be a consummation most devoutly to be wished. I have not yet heard, nor do I expect to hear, a voice raised in this hall to the contrary. . . .

Mr. Speaker, after what I have said upon this subject, you may perhaps be surprised to hear the declaration, that I am not at this session prepared to vote for any scheme of general emancipation. . . . But while I am unwilling to legislate definitely upon this subject, I am willing that the Committee to whom it was referred shall go on with their investigations—that they shall make their report to this House, that that report may go before the public, that the people may be brought to reflect upon it, and that a future Legislature may come here prepared to act definitively. . . .

(B) WM. DANIEL, JR., Campbell County

[*Richmond Enquirer*, Jan. 31, 1832.] Mr. DANIEL of Campbell, rose and said . . .

When the petitions from the county of Prince William were presented, I was one of the minority that opposed their reference. . . .

You may prove, if you can, that slavery is immoral, unjust and unnatural; that it originated in avarice and cruelty, that it is an evil and a curse, and you still do not convince me that our slaves are not property, and as such, protected by our Constitution. . . .

I would ask, then, why will you submit a proposition to the people, which carries upon its face a constitutional defect? . . .

Sir, much has been said about the miserable condition of our slaves. They have been represented as a poor, degraded, and wretched class of the community. If gentlemen will look to the condition of the poorer classes of society in those very countries, which have been held up to our view as bright examples of the prosperity and happiness that attend nations free from this blighting evil of slavery, which has been made the theme of so much eloquence in this House, they will find objects possessing much higher claims to their commiseration than the slaves in Virginia. . . . They are happy, and feelings of gratitude have, in most instances, attached them to us; and they would continue to be happy and to love us, if modern philanthropy did not use so many arguments to convince them that they are miserable, and ought to hate us as their oppressors. Show me, Sir, a happier man than one of those domestics, in the possession of a kind and indulgent owner. Proud of his master, he assumes his name, apes his manners, puts on his air of dignity, and is, as has been said by a most observant writer, "one of the veriest Aristocrats in the world." These remarks, it is true will not apply to most of them; but we confidently believe that a majority of them would look upon it as an act of cruelty on our part to break asunder the ties which bind them to their masters and their families, and send them unprovided for, to a strange and distant land. We too, Sir, are comparatively happy in the possession of them. . . .

(C) CHARLES J. FAULKNER, Berkeley County

[*The Speech of Charles Jas. Faulkner, (of Berkeley) in the House of Delegates of Virginia, on the Policy of the State with Respect to Her Slave Population. Delivered January 20* [sic], *1832, Richmond, 1832, p. 3.*] Mr. FAULKNER remarked . . .

[p. 8] Sir, resumed Mr. Faulkner, it is in the sense which I have above explained—not invidiously—not as a crusade against eastern principles and eastern interests, that I express my conviction that this question has become a measure of *vital policy with the west.* It is with us a necessary measure of self-defence. If we are to remain united as one people—and the gentleman from Dinwiddie has proclaimed *his* maxim to be "Virginia one and indivisible"—what my maxim may be sir, will depend upon events "which now cast their shadows before them." If we are to remain united, we must have some guarantee, that the evils under which you labor shall not be extended to us. . . .

Sir, what is our condition? *I mean the present condition of the* western portion of this commonwealth. I speak not as a theorist—I speak as to facts. Sir, the western part of this state now affords—or will, from the course of legislation adopted in our neighboring states, very shortly afford, the only outlet to your redundant and overflowing slave population. . . .

[p. 9] Sir, uniformity in political views, feelings and interests, in all the parts of this widely extended state, would, I admit, be extremely desirable. But that uniformity is purchased at too dear a rate, when the bold and intrepid forester of the west must yield to the slothful and degraded African—and those hills and vallies which until now have re-echoed with the songs and industry of freemen, shall have become converted into desolation and barrenness by the withering footsteps of slavery. Sir, our native, substantial, independent yeomanry, constitute our pride, efficiency and strength; they are our defence in war, our ornaments in peace; and no population, I will venture to affirm, upon the face of the globe, is more distinguished for an elevated love of freedom—for morality, virtue, frugality and independence, than the Virginia peasantry west of the Blue Ridge. Sir, may Heaven protect us from that curse, by which alone, so noble a race can be exterminated from their castles and inheritance!

[p. 10] . . . Sir, tax our lands—vilify our country—carry the sword of extermination through our now defenceless villages; but spare us, I implore you, spare us the curse of slavery—that bitterest drop from the chalice of the destroying angel.

Sir, the people of the west, I undertake to say, feel a deep, a lively, a generous sympathy for their eastern brethren. . . . Sir, we have lands, we have houses, we have property, and we are willing to pledge them all to any extent, to aid you in removing this evil. Yet, we will not, that you shall extend to us the same evils under which you labor. We will not that you shall make our fair domain, the receptacle of your mass of political filth and corruption. No, sir, before we can submit to such terms, violent convulsions must agitate this state. . . .

[p. 14] Sir, I would disdain, upon an occasion of this sort, appealing as it does to the fundamental principles upon which society is organized, to bandy with gentlemen, the petty technicalities of the law. My views are briefly these:—they go to the foundation upon which the social edifice rests. Property is the creature of civil society. The gentleman from Brunswick, and the gentleman from Dinwiddie, hold their slaves—not by any law of nature—not by any patent from God, as the latter gentleman on yesterday assumed—but solely by virtue of the acquiescence and consent of the society in which they live. So long as that property is not dangerous to the good order of society, it may and will be tolerated. But, sir, so soon as it does become pernicious—so soon as it is ascertained to jeopardize the peace, the happiness, the good order—nay, the very existence of society,—from that moment, the right by which they hold their property is gone. Society ceases to give its consent. The condition upon which they were permitted to hold it, is violated—their right ceases. This, sir, is the supreme law of society—a law above and paramount to all other laws—a law which cannot be questioned—which will not be denied.

Let me not be understood as assailing the *legal tenure* by which the slave holder claims his property. The law, it is true, has given to the master a right to his slaves—but it is a right subordinate to the GREAT *rights* of the community—and subject to that qualification which equally extends to every description of property, to wit: that it may be enjoyed so long as it is compatible with the public safety—but no longer. It is by virtue of the positive enactments of the state alone, that slaves are held as property, and pass in a regular course of distribution. If the time has now arrived, when the public interests demand a different course of legislation, the same power which made [p. 15] them property, can divest them of that quality. . . .

But, sir, it is said that society having conferred this property on the slave holder, it cannot *now* take it from him without an adequate compensation—by which is meant full value. I may be singular in the opinion, but I defy the legal research of the house to point me to a principle recognized by the law, even in the ordinary course of its adjudications, where the community pays for property, which is removed or destroyed because it is a nuisance and found injurious to that society. There is, I humbly apprehend, no such principle. . . . Sir, there is to my mind a manifest distinction between condemning private property to be applied to some beneficial public purpose, and condemning or removing private property which is ascertained to be a positive wrong to society. . . .

Sir, to contend that *full value* shall be paid for the slaves by the commonwealth, now or at any future period of their emancipation, is to deny all right of action upon this subject whatsoever. It is not within the financial ability of the state to purchase them. We have not the means. The utmost extremity of taxation would fall far short of an adequate treasury. What then shall be done? We must endea- [p. 16] vor to ascertain some middle ground of compromise between the rights of the community and the rights of the individual—some scheme, which, while it responds to the demands of the people for an extermination of the alarming evil, will not in its operation disconcert the settled institutions of society, or involve the slave holder in pecuniary ruin and embarrassment.

Sir, does not that plan of emancipation which proposes freedom at a future period—and which guarantees to the slave holder the present enjoyment and profit of that most pernicious species of property contain within itself a principle of compensation? a fair and just proposition of compromise? I think it does.

... [p. 17] Slavery, it is admitted, is an evil—it is an institution which presses heavily against the best interests of the state. It banishes free white labor—it exterminates the mechanic—the artizan—the manufacturer. It deprives them of occupation. It deprives them of bread. It converts the energy of a community into indolence—its power into imbecility—its efficiency into weakness. Sir, being thus injurious, have we not a right to demand its extermination? Shall society suffer, that the slave-holder may continue to gather his *crop* of human flesh? What is his mere pecuniary claim, compared with the great interests of the common weal? Must the country languish, droop, die, that the slave-holder may flourish? Shall all interests be subservient to one? all rights subordinate to those of the slave-holder? Has not the mechanic—have not the middle classes their rights?—rights incompatible with the existence of slavery? . . .

[p. 20] Sir, I am gratified to perceive that no gentleman has yet risen in this hall, the avowed advocate of slavery. The day has gone by, when such a voice could be listened to with patience, or even with forbearance. I even regret, sir, that we should find those amongst us, who enter the lists of discussion as its *apologists*, except alone upon the ground of uncontrollable necessity. And yet, who could have listened to the very eloquent remarks of the gentleman from Brunswick, without being forced to conclude, that he at least considered slavery, however not to be defended upon principle, yet as being divested of much of its enormity, as you approached it in practice.

Sir, if there be one, who concurs with that gentleman in the harmless character of this institution, let me request him to compare the condition of the slave-holding portion of this commonwealth—barren, desolate, and seared as it were by the avenging hand of heaven, with the descriptions which we have of this same country from those who first broke its virgin soil. To what is this change ascribable? Alone to the withering and blasting effects of slavery. If this does not satisfy him, let me request him to extend his travels to the northern states of this union—and beg him to contrast the happiness and contentment which prevails throughout that country—the busy and cheerful sound of industry—the rapid and swelling growth of their population—their means and institutions of education—their skill and proficiency in the useful arts—their enterprise, and public spirit—the monuments of their commercial and manufacturing industry; and, above all, their devoted attachment to the government from which they derive their protection, with the division, discontent, indolence and poverty of the southern country. . . .

(D) THOMAS MARSHALL, Fauquier County

[*The Speech of Thomas Marshall, (of Fauquier) in the House of Delegates of Virginia, on the Policy of the State in Relation to Her Colored Population: Delivered Saturday, January 14, 1832,* 2d ed., Richmond, 1832, p. 2.] MR. MARSHALL said . . .

[p. 3] In the present aspect of the case, he was constrained to vote against both the original resolution, and the substitute offered by the gentleman from Albemarle. Pursuing the order in which the vote must be taken, he would begin by stating his objections to the substitute.

The first and most satisfactory reason is, that the public mind is not prepared for the question of abolition. . . .

[p. 4] He objected to the substitute, in the second place, because it is too specific. . . .

This last consideration suggests the idea of a third objection to the substitute, namely, that the premature and unauthorized agitation of the measure is calculated to defeat the hope of its being adopted at any future time, and under circumstances more propitious. . . .

[p. 5] Again:—The ordinary condition of the slave is not such as to make [p. 6] humanity weep for his lot. Compare his condition with that of the laborer in any part of Europe, and you will find him blessed with a measure of happiness, nearly, if not altogether equal. He could say this, with great confidence, of that part of Virginia where he resided. The negro there is happy—he is treated with the most indulgent kindness—he is required to do the same work, and no more, than is performed by the white man—he is clothed with the best fabrics of the factories, and he is fed literally with the fat of the land. It is not for his sake, then, nor to meliorate his condition, that abolition is desirable. Wherefore, then, object to slavery? Because it is ruinous to the whites—retards improvement—roots out an industrious population—banishes the yeomanry of the country—deprives the spinner, the weaver, the smith, the shoemaker, the carpenter, of employment and support. The evil admits of no remedy. It is increasing, and will continue to increase, until the whole country will be inundated by one black wave, covering its whole extent, with a few white faces here and there floating on the surface. The master has no capital but what is vested in human flesh; the father, instead of being richer for his sons, is at a loss to provide for them. There is no diversity of occupations, no incentive to enterprise. Labor of every species is disreputable, because performed mostly by slaves. Our towns are stationary, our villages almost every where declining; and the general aspect of the country marks the curse of a wasteful, idle, reckless population, who have no interest in the soil, and care not how much it is impoverished. Public improvements are neglected; and the entire continent does not present a region for which nature has done so much, and art so little. If cultivated by free labor, the soil of Virginia is capable of sustaining a dense population, among whom labor would be honorable, and where "the busy hum of men" would tell that all were happy, and that all were free.

Mr. M. then proceeded to state his objections to the original resolution. . . .

[p. 9] But the question will be asked, what remedy do you propose for this growing evil? To this he would reply—strike at the annual increase of the colored population—endeavour to remove gradually as many of the blacks who are now free, and of those who may hereafter be emancipated for that purpose, as the resources of this great commonwealth will permit. Put your shoulder to the wheel, and then call on Hercules to help you. Invoke the aid of the United States, in the promotion of these objects and the ulterior one of purchase and deportation. Let every man retain his slave who wishes to keep him; and let the fund for transportation, or for purchase and removal, be exclusively under state control.

Some gentlemen direct their whole policy—or rather level their whole artillery, against the free blacks; and recommend a system of coercive measures, if persuasion should fail. . . . [p. 10] All that it seems necessary or proper to do in regard to the negroes now free, is to remove the annual increase. A sufficient number for this purpose will accrue from voluntary emigration, and from the power given to county courts to expel them when a burden to the community.

The annual increase of this class is computed at 1,200; that of slaves at 4,800;—and the annual removal of both classes, in that proportion, and to that amount, would have the double effect of preserving the ratio now existing between them, and of keeping the total amount of colored population at its present point, while the white would gradually, we may hope, rapidly increase. . . .

[p. 11] Auxiliary to this scheme, but not necessarily connected with it, is a plan for the purchase and removal of slaves. . . . Many masters are unable to give away their slaves, who would be content to sell them at a very reduced rate, perhaps at half price, for the benefit of the slaves themselves. . . .

But here again it will be asked, in what way shall the money be obtained for making these purchases? Sir, the proceeds of the public lands are at the disposal of congress. . . . [p. 12] But let not reliance be placed on this resource alone. Our citizens have asked that measures may be taken, for so amending the constitution of the United States, as to invest congress with the right of appropriating money for the removal of free negroes; and in some instances, the petitioners have required that the powers of congress should be so enlarged as to purchase and remove slaves likewise. . . .

FIFTH DAY, MONDAY, JANUARY 16, 1832

(For parliamentary movements on January 16 see p. 19.)

(A) WM. H. ROANE, Hanover County

[*Richmond Enquirer,* Feb. 4, 1832.] Mr. ROANE, of Hanover, said . . .

I know not, Sir, what are the wishes or opinions of my constituents on this subject. They did not, they would not tell me—they shall now know mine—I lay it down as a postulatum, that free white people, free blacks, and slave blacks cannot and ought not to constitute one and the same society. The reasons why they should not, are so obvious and well understood, that it would be but a waste of time to recite them. As a member of the Committee to whom this whole subject was referred, I contributed my humble mite towards the formation of a scheme to be presented to the House for removing, in the *first place* all free blacks from the Commonwealth. That done, Sir, *pari passu,* if means can be devised (and the able gentleman from Dinwiddie has proved that they can,) I am in favor, to the extent of those means of a *slow, gradual, certain,* and energetic system for the removal of all *emancipated* or *purchased* slaves from the Commonwealth, till the *ratio of population* between them and the whites, attains, at least, that equilibrium, which, in all future time, will give to every *white man* in the State, that *certain* assurance that *this* is *his* country; which every slave-holder should feel, and ever shall feel, as far as I am concerned, that his SLAVE IS HIS OWN PROPERTY. . . .

It is needless now to view this as an abstract question; to turn aside and enter into the metaphysical doctrines of the natural equality of man, or the abstract moral right of slavery. If I was to do so, I might shock the tender nerves of many good people; for I am not one of those who have ever revolted at the idea or practice of slavery, as many do. It has existed, and ever will exist, in all ages, in some form, and to some degree. I think slavery as much a correlative of liberty as cold is of heat. History, experience, observation, and reason, have taught me, that the torch of liberty has ever burnt brightest when surrounded by the dark and filthy, yet nutritious atmosphere of slavery. Nor do I believe in that Fan-faronade about the natural equality of man. I do not believe that all men are *by nature* equal, or that it is in the power of human art to make them so. I no more believe that the flat-nosed, woolly-headed black native of the deserts of *Africa*, is equal to the straight-haired white man of Europe, than I believe the stupid, scentless greyhound is equal to the noble, generous dog of *Newfoundland*. . . . Let us commence the work—let us barely enter the wedge, tap it lightly and gently, and leave it to posterity, (for none of us can be here,) to say whether *they* will drive it up to *abolition*. . . .

(B) RICE W. WOOD, Albemarle County

[*Richmond Enquirer*, Feb. 7, 1832.] Mr. WOOD of Albemarle, rose and said . . .

Mr. W. said that many facts had been stated, many arguments used, to convince us that Virginia has fallen from her high estate, and that the reason of all this is to be found in slavery, and in slavery alone. He said he was free to admit, that injurious consequences have resulted from slavery: that Virginia could not rival the Northern States in commercial wealth, in systems of education, internal improvements, or in manufactures. The true reason why she has not done so, he believed, would be found in other considerations. Had the early settlers of Virginia, like those who settled New England, been of that race of *Puritans* who fled from England and Scotland, because they were *there* denied the high privilege of worshipping their Creator according to the dictates of their conscience; and the principles of whose religion inculcated upon them, as a duty, abstemiousness from indulgences to the flesh; her condition might have been better without slaves. But the fact was far otherwise. The early settlers in Virginia were of the race of English gentlemen, many of them with large fortunes, who came to this delightful colony, not for the purpose of devoting themselves to lives of labour and self-denial; but for the purpose of enjoying the luxuries of the table, furnished alike from our forests and our waters. They came more to enjoy than to add to their wealth. They purchased large estates, erected palaces in the midst thereof, and devoted their time to the peaceful pursuit of agriculture. They did not vex themselves with the harrassing cares of commerce. They were not reduced to that hard necessity, which alone will force men to labour. They devoted themselves to social intercourse, to the cultivation of elegant literature and fine oratory. In these, they excelled not only any race of men in this Union, but perhaps in the world. . . .

Whilst I most ardently desire a remedy for that which I acknowledge to be an evil—yet there are certain principles which must be held sacred, in devising the remedy. One of these is, that the tenure by which this property is held must not be shaken. Another, that no man's property must be taken without his consent, unless compensation is made for it. A third, that we must first remove the free colored population. During this operation, or at its completion, manumission may be permitted, upon condition that the State has means ready for the immediate deportation of the manumitted. Under these qualifications, he would heartily co-operate in the consummation of [blurred] this great object. . . .

Such, Mr. W. said, were some of the views he entertained upon this subject, and the reasons and views herein set forth, had early led his mind to the conclusion, that any enactment at the *present*, touching slavery, would be unwise, perhaps pernicious—Unwise, 1st, because we have not been elected for this purpose; 2nd, because no definite opinion had been formed or expressed upon this subject; 3d, because no practicable or feasible scheme had yet been devised. . . .

(C) WM. B. PRESTON, Montgomery County

[*Richmond Enquirer*, Feb. 9, 1832.] Mr. PRESTON rose and said . . .

. . . This question of slavery, Mr. Speaker, is one which seems in all countries and ages in which it has ever been tolerated, either directly or indirectly, to have called to its aid a mystic sort of right, and a superstitious sort of veneration, that has deterred even the most intrepid mind from an investigation into the rights, and an exposure of the wrongs on which it has been sustained. . . . The most casual observer of passing events had long since been convinced that the West, if possible, should not be heard. . . . We will be heard. . . .

It was, therefore, that slaves which were not property by the common law, were made so by statutory enactments. . . . The power which this Legislature possessed of declaring what *shall be* property, also enables it to declare what *shall not* be property. All that I claim on this question, is, that when the public necessity demanding their emancipation is greater than the public necessity for their retention as slaves, that then it is in the power of this or any subsequent Legislature to repeal this statute. . . . I repeat again, Mr. Speaker, that no emancipation can take place either now or at any future time, without an infringement upon the rights of property, if they are such as are assumed on the other side—a right both to those now in existence and to those hereafter to be born, which is *superior to all law and above all necessity.* I see, Mr. Speaker, by indications that I cannot be mistaken in, that I have uttered a sentiment that gratifies those who are opposed to me. They are ready to accuse me with attacking their Constitutional rights. I do attack them openly, boldly; and if they ask me by what right I attack them, I answer by the right which is given me by that great law of necessity—*self-preservation;* which even by the gent. from Dinwiddie, (Gen. B.,) is said to be the supreme law of the land. The gentleman from Mecklenburg, (Mr. Goode,) shakes his head. I attack his property boldly, openly—let him defend it if he can. My old friend from Halifax, (Mr. Bruce) told us that the Virginia slave was happy and contented—that his situation was preferable to that of the labouring classes in Europe, and that no danger was to be apprehended. Mr. Speaker, this is impossible: happiness, is incompatible with slavery. The love of liberty is the ruling passion of man; it has been implanted in his bosom by the voice of God, and he cannot be happy if deprived of it. . . . The gentleman from Brunswick, (Mr. Gholson) after depicting in glowing colors the prosperous character of our country, the beauty of our daughters, the high and manly chivalry of our sons, concludes by telling us that the only wealth of Eastern Virginia was in the increase of their slaves. In the name of God, Mr. Speaker, has it come to this? Does the wealth and the beauty and the chivalry of Virginia derive its support and owe its existence to the increase of our slaves?—If it be so, Mr. Speaker, I would gladly relieve them of so heavy a reproach. . . .

SIXTH DAY, TUESDAY, JANUARY 17, 1832

(A) ALEX. G. KNOX, Mecklenburg County

[*Richmond Enquirer*, Feb. 11, 1832.] Mr. KNOX rose and said . . .

. . . Sir, I regard the conduct more than the opinions of men; and Mr. Jefferson presented a practical example, which cannot be mistaken: he never acted upon this mild and disinterested principle that gentlemen say he recommended to others, by liberating his slaves —but, Sir, continued in their possession, and perpetuated their condition by the last solemn act of his life; which is sufficient with me to put to flight all the conclusions that have been drawn from the expression of this abstract opinion. But, Sir, upon what principle is it that gentlemen have arrived at the conclusion, that slavery is this crying evil, this cormorant that is preying upon the vitals of the body politic, consuming all that is valuable in the principles of our Government?—Sir, I cannot agree with the gentlemen—I cannot force my mind, even by calling to its aid, humanity, religion or philanthropy, to the conclusion that slavery, as it exists in Virginia, is an evil. But, Sir, on the contrary, I consider it susceptible of demonstration that it is to this very cause, that we may trace the high and elevated character which she has heretofore sustained; and, moreover, that its existence is indispensably requisite in order to preserve the forms of a Republican Government. Sir, I would ask gentlemen to point to one solitary instance of a Government, since the institution of civil society, in which the principle of slavery was not tolerated in some form or other. Sir, from the very inherent nature of society, it has and will continue to exist. Fortune, genius and physical power, constitute a difference in men; and notwithstanding nature has drawn no line of distinction between him who drives, and him who rides within the coach; yet circumstances have; and these circumstances force the one to lend his services to the accommodation of the other. Sir, in the Republics of Greece and Rome, that have been denominated the cradles of liberty—from whose spirit millions have been awakened to the love of freedom, slavery was tolerated in the severest form, and the principle by which it was governed, relentless to every feeling of humanity. England, on whose soil the principle of universal emancipation first claimed its existence, contains a miserable, wretched and degraded peasantry, who perform the menial duties of life, compared to whom, our slaves may be regarded as occupying a most enviable condition. Humanity, Sir, must plead in vain for their removal. For, place it upon this ground, and none can hesitate to acknowledge, but that the slave in Virginia, reared as he is to the knowledge of moral principle, is in a more happy condition than the African, wandering as he does in ignorance and wretchedness, over the sun-scorched deserts of his native land, a stranger to the lights of moral or revealed religion. . . .

(B) GEO. W. SUMMERS, Kanawha County

[*Richmond Enquirer*, Feb. 14, 1832.] Mr. SUMMERS of Kanawha, rose and said . . .

I will not advert to the great principles of eternal justice, which demand at our hands the release of this people—I will not examine, here, the authority upon which one part of the human family assume the right to enslave the other—I will not open the great volume of nature's laws, to ascertain if it is written there that all men are alike in the sight of Him, who must regard with equal beneficence, the creatures of his hands, without distinction of color or condition. Apart from all these, every motive of policy and security requires that this question should be fairly and fully weighed, and that measures, cautious, but energetic in their character, gradual, but certain in their operations, should grow out of it, having for their object the final emancipation of the slaves of this Commonwealth, and their removal from our territory. I am no fanatic or philanthropic enthusiast, anxious only to better the condition of the blacks. On the contrary, I believe that, at the present day, the situation of the Virginia negro, so far as regards mere animal comfort, may be well compared with that of a large portion of the labouring classes in other countries, particularly in the severer governments of Europe. I know that many of them, perhaps the larger portion of them, are content with their destiny, and have furnished in frequent instances, rare examples of undying friendship, of grateful devotion and fidelity to those under whose control circumstances have placed them. It is to better our own condition, to arrest the desolating scourge of our country, to save from after ages the accumulated ills of a then hopeless and remediless disease, that we are now called upon to act. . . .

But as laborers, how inferior are slaves compared with a free, intelligent population. Their work is always performed in the worst possible manner, the natural result of a total want of interest in the mode of its execution, and the absence of intelligence to direct them if the interest existed. In many employments, they are almost useless. Knowledge is incompatible with slavery, and without knowledge, many of the occupations of life would cease. . . .

A slave population, exercising the most pernicious influence upon the manners, habits and character, of those among whom it exists. Lisping infancy learns the vocabulary of abusive epithets, and struts the embryo tyrant of its little domain. The consciousness of superior destiny, takes possession of his mind at its earliest dawning, and love of power and rule, "grows with his growth and strengthens with his strength." When, in the sublime lessons of christianity, he is taught to "do unto others as he would have others do unto him," he never dreams that the degraded negro is within the pale of that holy canon. Unless enabled to rise above the operation of powerful causes, he enters the world with miserable notions of self-importance, and under the government of an unbridled temper.

Habits of idleness, and their usual accompaniment, dissipation, are seldom avoided in a slave-holding community. . . . Men seldom labor when they can avoid it—labour becomes dishonorable, because it is the business of a slave—and when industry is made dishonourable or unfashionable, virtue is attacked in her strongest citadel. . . .

It will not be denied, I think, that slavery tends to diffuse ignorance among those more immediately in contact with it. I do not intend to assert that a location in a slave-holding community is incompatible, with the highest development of human intellect. Such a position would be controverted by facts. I know that the Southern States of our Union have, within the last fifty years, furnished a mass of genius and talent rarely equalled, never surpassed, in any age or country—our own good Commonwealth would unfold the long roll of her own immortal sons and point in silence to names which can never die. But, Sir, I speak in reference to the great body of the people, and ask you to compare the general distribution of elementary education in the non slave-holding with that in the slave-holding States. In a document recently examined, the number of persons in the State of Connecticut, unable to read, is stated at about thirty. I should blush to see the catalogue of my own State. I fear there is a multitude to whom even that volume, which is the history of our origin and the record of our redemption, is a "sealed book."

Where slavery prevails, the spirit of free inquiry and adventurous enterprize, is much repressed in the class to which I have alluded.— The difference is manifest even between the Eastern and Western parts of this Commonwealth. I speak not invidiously, for I am a native of the East. The remark, too, is founded partly upon the observation of Eastern gentlemen, who have been struck with this diversity. In that quarter, there is more equality, more freedom of thought and expression, more boldness of investigation, with the laboring class of our free population, than in the East. The poorest individual, if he has but a trusty rifle, a log cabin, and a "patch of corn," is the most independent of men. He knows nothing of slavery, scarcely even by example—he contributes his mite with cheerfulness to support his country in peace, and has a heart and an arm to aid her in the hour of danger. . . .

[*Richmond Enquirer,* Feb. 16, 1832.] At all times the NON-slave-holders of Virginia, are subjected to the most outrageous injustice by the presence of this population. To prevent, as far as may be, the mischiefs of insubordination, police laws have, from time to time, been enacted—the execution of which, for the most part, is thrown upon those who, themselves own none, of this property. In the character of PATROLS, they are made to perform onerous and disagreeable duties—not to protect themselves and their property, but to protect the slave-holder in the enjoyment of that which it is the interest of non-slave-holders, should not exist. He is thus made to fold to his own bosom, and protect the adder which stings him. . . .

The dangers to be apprehended from this population are multiplied by the increasing intelligence among them, the combined result of that general relaxation of treatment towards them, which none can have failed to observe, and the general diffusion of knowledge, which distinguishes the age in which we live. Men, to remain slaves, must remain ignorant. . . .

There is a continual and abiding danger of insubordination from the natural love of liberty, which the great Author of our being has imparted to all his creatures. It belongs to every thing which breathes the breath of life.—The imprisoned songster pants to plume his wings, and wanton in his native air—the caged lion seeks to rend the bars which confine him, and to range again the lord of the dark forest. It is a portion of the divine essence, which can never be wholly destroyed. Oppression cannot eradicate it. Amid the profoundest mental darkness, its feeble ray will sometimes light up the gloom within. It is a scintillation struck from the eternal rock of being, which can only be extinguished in the tomb. . . .

. . . We have never maintained that in Virginia, slaves are not property. However, founded in original outrage and injustice, however subversive of the great fundamental principles of a free people, I do not controvert the right of the present owner, to hold the slaves as his property—to hold him as such, so long as he may by force maintain his claim, and so long as he is permitted by the public good, and the public consent.

Sir, all property is held subordinate to, and only as it promotes the general welfare of, the community in which it exists. . . .

Mr. Speaker, by emancipating the *post nati,* the interests of the present owners are to be but little affected. . . .

Sir, the question was decided here, when the House referred the petitions from Hanover to the Select Committee. This is the act to which after time will trace the origin of American abolition. . . .

(C) JOHN A. CHANDLER, Norfolk County

[*The Speech of John A. Chandler, (of Norfolk County,) in the House of Delegates of Virginia, on the Policy of the State with Respect to Her Slave Population. Delivered January 17, 1832,* Richmond, 1832, p. 3.] Mr. CHANDLER rose and addressed the house as follows . . .

[p. 4] It has been said that this is the first session of the legislature which has ever admitted a discussion of this nature; and what, sir, does this prove? Clearly that there is no danger. . . . Do you require farther evidence of this? Look, sir, at the females who grace this auditory. The dimple of joy on their cheek, and the expression of mirth and happiness in their eye, attest there is no cause of alarm. And shall man, fearless man, whose boast and pride it is to be regardless of danger, shrink from the discussion of that, which woman, lovely woman, with all her tender sensibilities and timid apprehensions, smiles at? No, sir. . . .

[p. 5] The constitution of the United States has been quoted as authority in this debate, as of binding force in prohibiting our legislating upon this subject. . . . But it is said that the 5th article of the amendments to that constitution, which declares "that private property shall not be taken for public uses, without compensation," applies. This, sir, is a restraint imposed upon the *government of the United States,* by that article. . . .

[p. 6] The constitution of Virginia contains the identical provision mentioned in that of the United States, to wit: "that private property shall not be taken for public uses without just compensation;" and this has been quoted over and over again, and relied upon as conclusive, that the legislature cannot act in this matter. . . . The proposition, Mr. Speaker, is not whether the state shall take the slaves for public uses, but this: *whether the legislature has the right to compel the owners of slaves, under a penalty, within a reasonable time, to remove the future increase out of the country.* . . .

[p. 9] As other gentlemen, sir, have stated what they are willing to do, I consider it due to the house to declare how far I am prepared to go at present. I am not prepared to enact any LAW this session. I think we are not sufficiently acquainted with the sentiments of those we represent to justify us in acting definitively upon so great an extent of property. . . . [p. 10] I prefer a preamble, stronger and more expressive of this object, than the one which was offered by the gentleman from Goochland [*sic*] (Mr. Bryce,) but if I cannot get another more satisfactory, I shall vote for that, should it again be before the house.

SEVENTH DAY, WEDNESDAY, JANUARY 18, 1832

(A) JOHN T. BROWN, Town of Petersburg

[*The Speech of John Thompson Brown, in the House of Delegates of Virginia, on the Abolition of Slavery. Delivered Wednesday, January 18, 1832,* Richmond, 1832, p. 4.] MR. SPEAKER . . . It is useless to talk of avoiding *discussion.* It will be fortunate if we can prevent *action*—immediate and decisive action—on the subject of emancipation. . . .

. . . [p. 13] And sir, notwithstanding all that has been said to excite their apprehensions, do not the people of the west, perceive, in the peculiarities of their situation, satisfactory reasons for believing that slavery never will exist to any objectionable extent amongst them? The people of the east are planters. Slaves are the most suitable labourers for them. Any number of them may work to advantage together. Their labours are of a kind which white men are rarely found willing to engage in. The people of the west, on the other hand, are farmers and graziers. They need comparatively, but few labourers, and those only for certain periods of the year. White men can always be found for light and agreea- [p. 14] ble employments. The husbandman would prefer hiring to owning a man—because, upon a calculation of interest, he would rather pay a labourer for his work and let him go his way, than be burdened with his support throughout the year; whether wanting or not—and from the cradle to the grave. A few slaves there may be, in the west, to fill the menial, domestic offices, but they will never become the labourers of that region. . . . The foot of the negro delights not in the dew of the mountain grass. He is the child of the sandy desert. The burning sun gives him life and vigour, and his step is most joyous on the arid plain. Let the people of the west, be well assured, that in the peculiarities of their climate, their habits, feelings and pursuits—in the fixed and unalterable laws of nature—they have a more effectual *cordon sanitaire* than any with which legislative art can environ them. . . .

[p. 19] I have now examined all the schemes of emancipation which have been presented in the course of this debate; I have said nothing of the removal of people of color who are now free. That is a measure wholly independent of the one under consideration. It cannot with propriety be blended with it. Its very object is adverse, being intended as a means of enabling the slave owner to retain his property in safety and tranquility. . . .

Having arrived at the conclusion that emancipation is im- [p. 20] practicable, it would seem superfluous to pursue the subject further. Our deliberations, I humbly conceive, ought never to have been carried beyond this point. Of what avail is it to demonstrate that slavery is an evil, unless it can be shown that it is possible to get rid of it? . . .

And is there, then, no apology for slavery? Is it a sin of so deep a die that none dare vindicate it? For my own part sir, I am not the advocate of slavery in the abstract, and if the question were upon introducing it, I should be the very last to agree to it; but I am yet to be convinced, that slavery as it exists in Virginia, is either criminal or immoral. It was cast upon us by the act of others. It was one of the attendant circumstances under which we were ushered into life. [p. 21] It was a condition charged on the tenure of our existence. It is our lot, our destiny—and whether, in truth, it be right or wrong—whether it be a blessing or a curse, the moment has never yet been, when it was possible for us to free ourselves from it. This is enough to satisfy my conscience. . . .

[p. 22] This brief reference to the history of slavery, proves that it was forced upon us by a train of events that could not be controlled. Every effort was made to suppress it, and when that was no longer possible, effectual measures were taken to prevent its propagation elsewhere. What was brought upon us without our agency, and tolerated at first, from unavoidable necessity, has now become essential to our happiness, and is not inconsistent with that of the slave himself. In what code of ethics, human or divine, is it written that slavery is an offence of so odious a character that no circumstances can palliate it—no necessity excuse it? Whence is derived the authority for saying that it is a sin, so very foul and monstrous, that Virginia is bound to pluck it from her bosom, though her life's blood should gush after it? Sir, there are pure and holy men who have looked upon it without abhorrence. . . . The Savior of mankind did not condemn it. He appeared in a province of the Roman Empire, which was filled with slaves. . . . Christ saw these slaves—their numbers and their wretchedness. Nothing escaped his all-pervading eye. He came into the world to reprove sin, and he did reprove it, in all the diversified forms in which it appeared before him. Yet he rebuked not slavery. On the contrary, he gave it his implied approbation by exhorting masters to be kind to their servants —and enjoining it on servants to be faithful and obedient to their masters. Shall we, sir, affect a morality more pure and exalted than that of the primitive christians, or even the blessed author of our faith? . . .

[p. 23] Again, sir; I contend that the happiness of the slave does not call for his emancipation. His condition is better than that of four-fifths of the human family. He enjoys far more of the comforts of life, than the peasantry of many of the nations in Europe. . . . The slave also amasses nothing, but whatever betides, he is sure of a subsistence. He is independent of accident or the elements. If his owner becomes too poor to feed and clothe him, he is sure to sell him to one who is able. His life is under the protection of the law. When disabled by age or disease, he is secure of a support. Public opinion, and the interests of his master, protect him from cruel and abusive treatment. He is not free, but that is a blessing only in name, to a large majority of the human race. Man must be civilized, his mind enlightened, and his feelings refined, before he is fitted for the enjoyment of liberty. . . . [p. 24] The greater part of mankind must, in the nature of things, be poor and ignorant, toiling anxiously for their daily bread. All cannot be raised to the top of the scale; and the negro, of all others, is the least susceptible of elevation. . . .

[p. 25] But, it is urged with vehemence, that our interests require the removal of slavery. I confess, sir, if there be any consideration which calls for it, this to my mind, carries with it the most weight. And yet it is certain, that whatever evils may flow from slavery, it would now be a far greater evil to abolish it. The sombre pictures which have been drawn of the deplorable condition of the commonwealth, are in a great measure, imaginary—and so far as they are true, the causes have been mistaken. . . . [p. 26] Why then is Virginia poor, and in debt? Not, sir, because she has nothing for market, but because she is defrauded in the sale of her produce and the purchase of her supplies from abroad. . . . The northern states import all the goods, and we of the south buy our supplies from them. They act both as merchants and carriers, and in that combined character, engross the whole commercial profit. It is this annual tribute to the north, superadded to enormous duties on imports, that keeps the south poor; and it is this same tribute which makes the north rich, and builds up those splendid mansions and cities of which we have heard so much in this debate.

[p. 27] Again, it is said that slavery retards the increase of white population, and for proof of the position we are referred to the comparatively rapid growth of the western states, which is ascribed to the non-existence of slavery in them. . . . The only fair criterion is a comparison between the slave holding and non-slave holding states, similarly situated, on the seaboard, and which may be presumed to have contributed alike to the peopling of the west. . . . The ratio of increase of whites in Virginia, is fifteen per cent.; in Delaware it is less than six per cent.; in New Jersey fifteen; in Massachusetts sixteen, and in the far-famed Connecticut, only eight per cent.! Can there be a remaining suspicion, that slavery has caused emigration from Virginia, or in any manner checked her population? . . .

[p. 28] . . . The only subject of inquiry at present is, as to the ratio of increase of *slaves*. . . . [p. 29] The important fact to which I wish to direct your attention, is, that although the number of slaves has gained on that of the whites since 1790, yet that the ratio of that gain has been rapidly diminishing for the last twenty years, and is now almost extinguished. At one time, it was as eleven to one—it is now as nine to eight. It is said, however, that we have heretofore had an outlet for a considerable portion of our slaves in the southern states—that they are now about to close their doors, and of course that drain must cease. . . . They have passed such laws before, and repealed them. They will repeal them again. They will be evaded even whilst in force. . . .

. . . [p. 31] And if you pass an act that violates the right of property in slaves, it will be met with the sharp, quick remedy of resistance; it will shake this ancient commonwealth to its centre; it will sever it in twain. . . .

(B) SAMUEL M. GARLAND, Amherst County

[*Richmond Enquirer*, April 17, 1832.] Mr. GARLAND rose and said . . .

. . . Upon the abstract question, whether one man has the right to hold his fellow-man in bondage, he had not a word to say. No man has been found sufficiently bold to come forward here, as the advocate of slavery in the abstract. The principles of our free institutions, the spirit of the times in which we live, the genius of liberty which is now walking abroad over the earth, would alike denounce such a doctrine as odious and abominable; and he trusted its advocate would not be found in this Republic, so famed in revolutionary history for its attachment to the unalienable rights of man, and for the many sacrifices it made in that glorious struggle. . . .

The evils of slavery have again and again been presented in bold relief to the notice of the House. . . . In the May-day of life, she [Virginia] wears upon her countenance the evidence of premature decay, and the yellow leaf of Autumn has followed too soon the budding blossoms of Spring. And to what known cause can this be assigned, but to the existence of slavery,—this cancer which destroys at the fountain, the streams of vigorous and healthful existence? Her citizens are as industrious, as moral, and as talented, as those of any other State, and her natural resources are surpassed by none. Yet, all these gifts that have been lavished upon her, and all the energies of her sons have, in a great degree, been lost and paralyzed by this national calamity. Like a pestilence, it has swept over our land, withering and blighting whatever it breathed upon. . . .

EIGHTH DAY, THURSDAY, JANUARY 19, 1832

(A) GEORGE I. WILLIAMS, Harrison County

[*Richmond Enquirer*, April 24, 1832.] Mr. WILLIAMS of Harrison, rose and said . . .

The remarks of several gentlemen upon an expression of mine at an early period of the session, demand that I should revert to it. It has been said that I gave to my brethren from the East, a *carte blanche* on this subject. I do not deny the expression. But I do repel the use which has been made of it.—They have argued that I pledged myself and those who act with me, to refrain from any participation in the deliberations of this body upon the subject of slavery—to a passive acquiescence in whatever they might do; and even bound myself to be content, should they unwisely decide to do nothing.—Not so, Mr. Speaker. I had no intention of acting so pliant a part. The gentleman from Dinwiddie had then declared, with impressive solemnity, that "something must be done;" he had exhibited in strong language, the condition of the Eastern country, under the influence of that rational terror which the Southampton insurrection had inspired. And, sympathizing in the misfortunes of our brethren, I declared my determination to aid them in some corrective measure—to throw no obstacles in the way of any plan which they, as the party most interested, should devise for their relief and safety. So far I was then willing to go—so far I will go now—and with such sentiments I gave them a *carte blanche*.—But how have they used the proffered kindness—have they filled up the blank? I did not dream that it would be returned to me with a protest against its use—but such is the fact. They have lauded my generosity, while I thought only of justice. . . .

[*Richmond Enquirer*, April 27, 1832.] Unsatisfied—as well they may be—of the strength of the argument that man possesses the natural right to hold his fellow in bondage, the gentlemen from Petersburg and Dinwiddie go for that right to the laws—they tell us that slaves are property under the statute. They are forced to abandon any pretensions to constitutional right, and settle down upon their sole defence—the right under the statute. Reduced to this point, the argument presents no difficulty—for, if statutory provisions alone give the right, then, *eo nomine*, it may be taken away, by the power existing in the legislature to repeal the statutes. But the gentleman from Petersburg has added to the guarantee of slave property, "the common consent and usage of the country," a defence still more liable to be withdrawn. For if the common consent ceases, the protection which it gave, while in existence is abrogated instanter: And to that event, present circumstances point with unerring correctness.

Perhaps one of the most remarkable arguments in the whole course of the debate, was that by which the gentleman from Petersburg, (Mr. Brown,) endeavored to maintain that our slaves do not wish to be liberated—that servitude is sweet; and that the yoke and the fetter sit as lightly on their limbs, as garlands of flowers and wreaths of palm. The gentleman was led away by his exuberant imagination, into a picture of patriarchal simplicity and passionless content, which exists only in the dreams of fancy. That gentleman knows the human heart too well to blind himself to the influence of its passions and aspirations. The poorest tattered negro, who tills the planter's field, under his task-master, and labors to produce those fruits which he may never call his own, feels within him that spark which emanates from the deity—the innate longing for liberty,—and hears in the inmost recesses of his soul, the secret whisperings of nature, that tell him he should be free. The love of freedom is a universal animal principle—it is concomitant with vitality. No human being was ever born without the wish for liberty implanted in his breast. God never made a slave—for slavery is the work of man alone. The prisoned bird flutters against the bars of his narrow cage, and pants for the shades of his native wild-wood, and the breath of his native sky. . . .

The gentleman has also alluded to our Saviour, and declares that the Redeemer gave a negative countenance to slavery, by omitting it in the enumeration of crimes, and by having often spoken of the relations between master and servant, all servants being then slaves, without reprobating the holding of slaves as a crime. But I agree, Mr. Speaker, that the Saviour did not come into the world to teach us politics of municipal regulations; but to offer himself as a sacrifice for the transgressions of men. He spoke, it is true, after the manner of men, and so did Joshua, when he bade the sun to stand still. But the gentleman very well knows that it was the earth, and not the sun, whose motion was arrested.—From these facts, it is plain that the Bible does not afford either a system of astronomy or politics quite suited to the present time. . . .

(B) JOHN E. SHELL, Brunswick County

[*Constitutional Whig*, Feb. 16, 1832.] Speech of Mr. SHELL of Brunswick. . . .

Mr. Speaker, I was a soldier in this war [the Southampton Insurrection]—not a hero—mark that—not a hero. It is not impossible that I might have acquired renown, but for the unfortunate intervention of one of those accidental incidental casualties which so frequently impede the march of fame, and check the aspirations of ambition. My prospect to win a laurel, was blighted by the smallest imaginable circumstance. Sir, dreadful as it is, I must tell you that, just before we reached the scene of action, *three men and two boys* encountered this mighty General, and his *formidable* army, and literally demolished them—defeated them "horse, foot and dragoons" —and scattered death and confusion among them. . . .

... There were not two or three, but repeated instances, in which escape, and narrow escape was effected by the timely, voluntary assistance, and information of slaves....

[*Constitutional Whig*, Feb. 24, 1832.] Mr. SPEAKER: I have attempted to shew to this House, that whatever the evils of slavery may be—whatever the dangers which accompany its existence—whatever the calamities it is likely to bring upon our country, our pecuniary condition and prospects are such as to render action now totally impracticable....

... Removals, and many removals, have certainly taken place from the section to which our attention has been directed. Not, sir, I assure you to escape the evil and curse of slavery. The emigrant, so far as my observation extends, almost invariably settles again among a slave population; generally in the rich vallies of the West, where he can enjoy greater facilities to market, and reap the full harvest of more abundant agricultural production. The march of empire is to the West....

The gentleman [Faulkner], in order, I suppose, to stimulate us to action, told us that his course in relation to a *division* of *the State*, would depend on future events. By this declaration, we are left to infer, that should his efforts in the cause of abolition fail, then he will go for division.... But I take this opportunity to say, in the language of truth, that if this question be carried against us, it will immediately be met by a proposition to *divide this State*....

NINTH DAY, FRIDAY, JANUARY 20, 1832

(A) THOMAS J. RANDOLPH, Albemarle County

[*The Speech of Thomas J. Randolph, (of Albemarle,) in the House of Delegates of Virginia, on the Abolition of Slavery: Delivered Saturday, Jan. 21* [sic], *1832*, 2d ed., Richmond, 1832, p. 4.] MR. SPEAKER ...

I will make a single remark to correct an erroneous impression, which has arisen from an expression used the other day by my friend from Campbell, (Mr. Rives,) "that this was the plan of Mr. Jefferson." It has been understood as conveying the idea that Mr. Jefferson had left a fully developed plan of abolition: this is not the fact. The idea is contained in his published works. I cannot now tell whether I received it from them, or from the impressions of social intercourse, probably from both: the impression has long been deeply imbued in my mind. If in the resolution there is one suggestion worthy of notice, be the honour to him; whatever is objectionable, be the odium and disgrace upon my head....

... [p. 6] I cannot concur in the views of gentlemen who distrust the people; who fear them; and who will not submit to their decision in this matter.—Great reprobation has been thrown upon this plan, because it is said to contain no guarantee for property. The resolution does not prescribe the condition upon which it shall become the property of the commonwealth. Whether by the surrender of such portions as are not removed within the time specified—whether by payment for it at birth, at its full value, or at a reduced average, or such portions of it at this age, as the funds of the commonwealth would justify, to be apportioned in such manner as may be provided by law, to be left with the masters of their mothers until their services shall have paid the expense of rearing, or in any other manner that the wisdom of this house should direct. . . . As they [gentlemen] have said so much about the property feature, I will take a passing notice of it. I do not concur in the abstract opinions of the gentlemen of the West. I cannot concur with the hopeless, ultra absolutism of the South. . . .

... [p. 7] Yet, sir, you will not allow the non-slaveholder to vote in the decision touching that property whose benefits I acknowledge he does not participate, but in whose inconveniences and perils he has more than his full share. It is well known that it has been the practice, if not the policy of the large slaveholder, to make the poor man the instrument of their police and their punishments to their slaves; which has begotten hostility between the slave and the less wealthy, that makes their condition the most perilous in all insurrectionary movements. . . .

[p. 9] The gentleman has objected to the West deciding this question.—He has again misconstrued the resolution. It is, or intended to be permissive and not obligatory, upon the subsequent legislature. . . .

... [p. 11] The gentleman from Petersburg, (Mr. Brown,) and the gentleman from Brunswick, have spoken with much exultation of what they are pleased to call the decrease of the ratio of the colored population since 1790. Since 1790, the blacks have increased upon the whites in East Virginia, 106,000. There was a regular increase of the ratio from 1790 to 1820. The ratio is now, in the whole state, one-third of one per cent. less than in 1790; and this has been effected by the revulsion of prices of 1819, which threw thousands of slaves upon the market in the following years, and swept over the land with the devastation of a tornado, uprooting the proudest oaks, and breaking the noblest hearts. May God in his mercies avert a reduction by similar means. . . .

[p. 14] I agree with gentlemen in the necessity of arming the state for internal defence. I will unite with them in any effort to restore confidence to the public mind, and to conduce to the sense of the safety of our wives and our children. Yet, sir, I must ask upon whom is to fall the burden of this defence; not upon the lordly masters of their hundred slaves, who will never turn out except to retire with their families when danger threatens. No, sir, it is to fall upon the less wealthy class of our citizens; chiefly upon the non-slaveholders. I have known patrols turned out when there was not a slaveholder among them, and this is the practice of the country. I have slept in times of alarm quietly in bed without having a thought of care, while these individuals owning none of this property themselves, were patrolling under a compulsory process, for a pittance of seventy-five cents per twelve hours, the very curtilage of my house, and guarding that property, which was alike dangerous to them and myself. . . .

. . . [p. 15] The gentleman has spoken of the increase of the female slaves being a part of the profit: it is admitted; but no great evil can be averted, no good attained, without some inconvenience. It may be questioned, how far it is desirable to foster and encourage this branch of profit. It is a practice, and an increasing practice in parts of Virginia, to rear slaves for market. How can an honorable mind, a patriot, and a lover of his country, bear to see this ancient dominion, rendered illustrious by the noble devotion and patriotism of her sons in the cause of liberty, converted into one grand menagerie where men are to be reared for market like oxen for the shambles. Is it [p. 16] better, is it not worse, than the slave trade, that trade which enlisted the labor of the good and the wise of every creed and every clime to abolish it? . . . [p. 17] The gentleman has appealed to the Christian religion in justification of slavery. I would ask him upon what part of those pure doctrines does he rely; to which of those sublime precepts does he avert to sustain his position? Is it that which teaches charity, justice and good will to all, or is it that which teaches "that ye do unto others as ye would they should do unto you?" . . .

(B) WILLOUGHBY NEWTON, Westmoreland County

[*Constitutional Whig*, Feb. 14, 1832.] When Mr. RANDOLPH had concluded his speech—Mr. NEWTON rose and spoke to the following effect:

Mr. SPEAKER . . .

Sir, the people sent us here to represent them—to do that for them which they cannot so well accomplish for themselves; and when any great question arises, if we shrink from the responsibility that devolves upon us, and refer it to our constituents for decision, we had as well abandon our trust at once—leave the power of making laws with themselves, and no longer amuse them with the mockery of a representative government.

I wish it to be distinctly understood, here, and elsewhere, that it was in this sense that I denounced democracy. Not that I wished to impair the rights of the people, or to abridge their privileges in the slightest degree. On the contrary, it was my earnest desire to protect these rights and privileges; that prompted me to the course that I have pursued. . . .

But, sir, admit for the sake of argument, that it is proper upon some occasions, to abandon the representative principle, and to submit questions of great and momentous interest immediately to the people, for decision, I ask the gentleman from Albemarle, and this House, if this is the question which, of all others, should be selected for this great experiment? . . . The hustings—the muster ground— nay, sir, every crossroad and grog-shop, will be made the scene of angry debate, and noisy declamation, upon this agitating subject. What must be the inevitable consequence? Need I say what every gentleman must perceive—revolt and insurrection among our slaves. . . .

I do not propose to enter upon the boundless field of speculation in which gentlemen have roamed so much at large. Nor, sir, shall I attempt to answer the arguments of gentlemen who maintain that our property is not our own—that slaves are not property. I mean no disrespect to the gentlemen who have urged these arguments; but, sir, I would as soon attempt to convince, by argument, the midnight assassin, that my life is my own—or the highway robber that my purse is my property. Sir, it is not a question for argument. [Mr. PRESTON rose, and denied that he had ever maintained that slaves were not property.] Mr. NEWTON proceeded. What, then, is the gentleman's argument? Slaves are not such property as is protected by the Constitution, because they are made property by statute. Now, sir, I beg to be informed by what other title any other property in this Commonwealth is held? It is true that your lands and personal goods were property at the common law, and are regulated by the rules of the common law. But, I ask him, did the common law of England become the law of Virginia but by statute? . . .

(C) HENRY BERRY, Jefferson County

[*The Speech of Henry Berry, (of Jefferson,) in the House of Delegates of Virginia, on the Abolition of Slavery* (n.p., n.d.), p. 2.]

MR. BERRY rose and addressed the house. Mr. Speaker—Coming from a county in which there are about 4000 slaves, being myself a slave-holder; and I may say further, that the largest interest in property that I have in Virginia, lies about 100 miles east of the Blue Ridge, and consists of land and slaves—under these circumstances, I hope I shall be excused by my eastern brethren, for saying a few words on this important, and deeply interesting subject. That slavery is a grinding curse upon this state, I had supposed would have been admitted by all, and that the only question for debate here, would have been, the *possibility* of removing the evil. But, sir, in this I have been disappointed. I have been astonished to find that there are advocates here for slavery, with all its effects. . . .

. . . [p. 3] Pass as severe laws as you will, to keep these unfortunate creatures in ignorance, it is in vain, unless you can extinguish that spark of intellect which God has given them. Let any man who advocates slavery, examine the system of laws that we have adopted (from stern necessity it may be said,) towards these creatures, and he may shed a tear upon that, and would to God, sir, the memory of it might thus be blotted out forever. Sir, we have, as far as possible closed every avenue by which light might enter their minds; we have only to go one step further—to extinguish the capacity to see the light, and our work would be completed; they would then be reduced to the level of the beasts of the field, and we should be safe; and I am not certain that we would not do it, if we could find out the necessary process—and that under the plea of necessity.
. . . [p. 4] Sir, the right of property in the colored class generally, has been brought into this debate, and I am sorry for it; it is not to be treated in the abstract. But I think our eastern brethren are to blame for it; they rather arrogantly advance their right of property, as an insuperable barrier to our doing any thing for the removal of the evil of slavery, and rather challenged an investigation of their title, and it has been rather rudely handled in this debate. Yet, sir, I am for maintaining the bonds by which we hold this property *now*, with firmness and with vigilance; because it is necessary to the public safety that we should do so, and because there are vested rights to this property, under the law as it now is. Sir, I should be glad that this house should declare unanimously, that the relations between master and slave should not now be disturbed, that none of the present generation should be removed, except those who may be given up voluntarily. But, sir, the plea of *necessity* will not answer in bar to a scheme for the future gradual emancipation and removal of this class—that measure is within our power. . . . Sir, I am sick with the clamor in this debate, about this property, this wealth. I

consider it all as mere trash, when weighed against the public safety. The right of property in slaves, is entirely the creature of the positive law; all our rules of property are under the control of the legislature; our law of descents, distribution, &c. can be altered by the legislature whenever it shall seem expedient; and *a fortiori,* can the legislature alter the rule with regard to property in slaves, because the right is purely the creature of the legislature. . . . [p. 7] The gentleman gave us a long statistical statement, the object of which was to prove that slave labor is more productive than free labor. I presume that the exports from the city of New Orleans, formed a part of the estimate he gave us of southern exports. And sir, the fact that New Orleans is the shipping port for the western part of Pennsylvania, the western part of Virginia, the states of Ohio, Kentucky, Indiana, in fact, for almost the whole of the young and mighty west, destroys the whole force of his statement. . . . [p. 8] What stimulus has the slave to work, other than the lash? He argues thus: why should I fatigue myself with work? I am bound to work all my life—I reap not the fruits of my labor—I increase not my comfort by increasing my labor. What motive have I to save? My master is bound to provide for me as long as I live; he gets all the fruits of my labor—hence his whole policy is to work as little as possible, and to consume as much as possible—to save nothing. . . .

TENTH DAY, SATURDAY, JANUARY 21, 1832

(A) JAS. M'DOWELL, Rockbridge County

[*Speech of James M'Dowell, Jr. (of Rockbridge,) in the House of Delegates of Virginia, on the Slave Question: Delivered Saturday, January 21, 1832,* 2d ed., Richmond, 1832, p. 3.] MR. SPEAKER . . .

. . . [p. 4] So far as the debate has come within my knowledge, no direct inquiry has been made into the relative capacities of the negro and the white man, as *laborers*—as the mere agents of production. This inquiry seems to have been estopped by the general, I believe, universal concession, that slavery was an "evil." Thus, sir, a branch, necessary to the full investigation of the subject, and one upon which the expediency of a gradual emancipation can well be supported, has been indirectly closed. I say well supported, because no proposition can be more easily or conclusively established, both by general deduction from the principles of human nature, and by observed facts, than *this*, that the labor of a free white man, in the temperate latitude of Virginia, is more productive than that of a slave —yielding a larger aggregate for public and for private wealth. . . .

[p. 5] Your committee, sir, declare that legislation *"at present is inexpedient:"* The amendment proposed, and now under discussion, declares the contrary. Believing that the amendment takes the true ground, I shall endeavor to sustain it. . . .

[p. 9] . . . Our interests and senses, proclaim the progress of general decline; conscience and experience attest that slavery is its principal cause. Is it not so? When we look at Virginia as a whole, without pausing upon the bright and the beautiful that still show forth as intrinsic qualities *of her character*, but look at her, in reference to her every day practical habit and appearance, is she not any thing but prosperous? . . .

[p. 12] . . . It has been frankly and unequivocally declared from the very commencement of this debate by the most decided enemies of abolition themselves as well as by others—that this property is an "evil"—that it is a dangerous property. Yes, sir, so dangerous has it been represented to be even by those who desire to retain it, that we have been reproached for speaking of it otherwise than in fireside whispers—reproached for entertaining debate upon it in this Hall, and the discussion of it with open doors and to the general ear, has been charged upon us as a climax of rashness and folly which threatens issues of calamity to the country. . . .

[p. 15] The rights of private property and of personal security exist under every government, but they are not *equal*. Security is the primary purpose for which men enter into government; property, beyond a sufficiency for natural wants, is only a secondary purpose. It is because private property ministers to the uses and comforts and enjoyments of persons that it is sanctioned by law, and it is for these ends and these only that it is sanctioned. To these ends, therefore, must it be kept constantly subordinate, constantly conformed. When it loses its utility—when it no longer contributes to the personal benefits and wants of its holder in any equal degree with the expense or the risk or the danger of keeping it—much more—when it jeopards the security of the public—when this is the case, then the original purpose for which it is authorized is lost; its character of property, in the just and beneficial sense of it, is gone, and it may be regulated, without private injustice, in any manner which the general good of the community, by whose laws it was licensed, may require. . . .

[p. 16] Sir, this *"supreme law"* of the public safety which is thought to arise only when a State is in actual jeopardy of life and limb and which is then so plenary for all the purposes of defence—this law is best understood when it is believed to possess preventive as well as remedial agencies. . . .

[p. 17] After this argument it may be unnecessary to say, that there is in my judgement nothing wrong in the *post nati* or after-born principle which has been presented on this subject, by the gentleman (Mr. Randolph) from Albemarle. I decline, however, expressing any opinion, none being called for, as to the terms or manner in which he proposes to carry that principle into effect. . . .

[p. 18] We have been told in the course of this debate, frequently told, that the attachment of the slave to his owner is common, that, in numerous instances, it is warm and devoted, and the fact has been urged in reprehension of the idea that he cared for his freedom. The fact is undoubtedly true and it is one of honorable import to the humanity of our people. But although true it is only so in particular instances; the instances themselves are anomalous; they are out of the ordinary course of human nature; are in contradiction of its strongest passions; its leading principles and are chiefly noticeable for their novelty. Were we to assume isolated instances of this kind as instances upon [p. 19] which it would be just to construct a system of laws for the government and condition of the slave, our legislation would be a nullity; it would provide for the units of that population but let the mass of it escape. If, however, the fact in this case, be broad as it has been stated, and the inference from it—that freedom is no boon which is desired by the slave—be just, why, then, censure our debates upon this subject? Why censure us for holding out to the slave an unattainable object, for exciting impracticable hopes, for stimulating daring and incendiary attempts to accomplish them? One or the other of these judgements upon the temper and the wishes of the slave must be mistaken; being contrary they cannot both be true, but as both have furnished a separate ground of argument against us, from one at least, of these arguments we should be held as fairly discharged.

As to the idea that the slave, in any considerable number of cases, can be so attached to his master and his servitude as to be indifferent to freedom, it is wholly unnatural—rejected by the conscious testimony of every man's heart and by the written testimony of the world's experience. The truth is, sir, that although there are special instances of slaves who are willing to forego the benefits of *complete* freedom for certain other benefits which they enjoy under a *nominal* slavery, yet the instances, from their very nature, must be limited—they can extend only to a favored few and they furnish no authority for a decision upon the conduct of others. Take the slave in his general relation to ourselves, and you cannot regard him otherwise than as man,—having the capacities and resentments of man, both indeed repressed but both existing. Here, at least, in our country, he is not spurned from this distinction: humanity admits him as a member—soiled in his character and degraded in his fortunes, indeed, yet still a member of a common race and still entitled, as such, to our sympathy and kindness. This sentiment tells upon his condition here: you read it in his dwelling, you read it in his health, you read it in the quantum of his labor—in the manifold personal privileges which he enjoys. It is true, sir, to the letter, what gentlemen have frequently declared, that there is no laboring peasantry in any other part of the world, who, in all external respects, are better situated than our slave—who suffer less from want—who suffer less from hardship—who struggle less under the toils of life or who have a fuller supply of the comforts which mere physical nature demands. In all these respects he shares in the equalizing and benignant spirit of our institutions and our age. He is not the victim of cruelty—rarely, if ever, of oppression—is governed by an authority, which year after year, is abating of its harshness and is admitted to every privilege which the deprivation of his liberty can allow.

But, sir, it is in this very circumstance, in this alleviated and improved condition, that we have a principal cause of apprehension from the slave. You raise his intelligence with his condition, and as he better understands his position in the world, he were not man if it did not the more inflame his discontent. That it has this effect we all know; for the truth is proverbial, that a slave is the more unhappy as he is the more indulged. He could not be otherwise; he follows but the impulse of human nature in being so. . . .

. . . [p. 20] Sir, you may place the slave where you please—you may dry up, to your uttermost, the fountains of his feeling, the springs of his thought—you may close upon his mind every avenue of knowledge and cloud it over with artificial night—you may yoke him to your labors as the ox which liveth only to work and worketh only to live—you may put him under any process which, without destroying his value as a slave, will debase and crush him as a rational being—you may do this and the idea that he was born to be free will survive it all. It is allied to his hope of immortality—it is the ethereal part of his nature which oppression cannot reach; it is a torch lit up in his soul by the hand of the Deity and never meant to be extinguished by the hand of man. . . .

. . . [p. 23] In the midst of this general uncertainty, however, there is one thing which we can foresee with precision—one thing which we may be said to know. It is this, sir, *that the slave-holding interest of the country, will and can coalesce with no other interest and must, as a consequence, be separate and hostile to all others.* . . .

[p. 29] Was it the fear of Nat Turner and his deluded and

drunken handful of followers which produced or could produce such effects? Was it this that induced distant counties where the very name of Southampton was strange, to arm and equip for a struggle? No sir, it was the suspicion eternally attached to the slave himself, the suspicion that a Nat Turner might be in every family, that the same bloody deed could be acted over at any time in any place, that the materials for it were spread through the land and always ready for a like explosion. . . .

ELEVENTH DAY, MONDAY, JANUARY 23, 1832

(A) JOHN C. CAMPBELL, Brooke County

[*Constitutional Whig*, Jan. 24, 1832.] On motion of Mr. HALYBURTON, the House resumed the consideration of the Report of the Select Committee and Mr. PRESTON's amendment thereto.

Mr. MCDOWELL addressed a few words of explanation to the House.

Mr. HALYBURTON, took the floor and justified slavery, and depreciated its dangers, by the example of ancient nations.

[*Constitutional Whig*, March 16, 1832.] Mr. CAMPBELL of Brooke, said . . .

Sir, I would have the West to act, and act with firmness. I would have them as a body, to stand in the gap to entrench themselves in the fastness of their mountains, and never give an inch to the advancing enemy. I would even sever the unity of the State before I would tolerate the introduction of this evil. . . .

. . . Our opponents, themselves, with a few exceptions, admit the expediency of some measures calculated to reduce the evil. It is true, they do not admit it in direct terms; but in the character of their arguments, all of which are comprised in two main propositions—1st, We are constitutionally prohibited from all legislation upon the subject; 2d, If not so, still our situation is irremediable—abolition is impracticable. It is said, however, by some, that the situation of the country does not require any legislative movements on this subject—that no danger exists; that the country is quiet and prosperous; that the agitation of the subject at present, grows alone out of what is now called the "petty affair of Southampton." Are these averments true? . . . If no danger exists, why do these gentlemen tremble at our discussion? . . .

[*Constitutional Whig*, March 20, 1832.] It has been said, that this subject was introduced here, merely by an inconsiderate reference of a petition from a few fanatical Quakers. Sir, that is not correct. As a member of the Select Committee, to whom the subject was referred, I noted closely all the petitions which came before us, and the order in which they were presented. On the 7th, 8th and 9th of December, petitions from the counties of Fauquier, Page and Augusta, were referred, each, amongst other things, distinctively asking an action in aid of the *removal of slaves*.—The petition of the Friends was not presented until the 14th, so that this House had assumed jurisdiction of the subject before this much abused, but humble, petition of a most worthy portion of the good people of this Commonwealth had, perhaps, even reached this city. Again, sir, at the time this discussion commenced, there were on the table of the Select Committee, petitions on the same subject from no less than eleven counties, (seven Eastern and four Western,) and still it is said that the public voice has not called for our present deliberations; that all the good or evil of this discussion is due to the petitioning Friends. . . .

. . . The gentleman from Albemarle, (Mr. Randolph,) has stated to this House, that in a certain district of his county, 7 miles square, the entire population, save one old bachelor, awaits but our decision, to determine their removal. In other sections of the State, we are assured that similar feelings and determinations exist to a great extent. . . .

. . . Although anxious for the abolition of this *curse*, I am not of a temperament sufficiently sanguine to expect or believe that any bill could be reported which should be passed into a law during the present session. Still, sir, I desire the adoption of the amendment now before us—the effect of which will be, an instruction to the Committee to prepare and report to this House, the best scheme they can devise. . . .

TWELFTH DAY, TUESDAY, JANUARY 24, 1832

(A) WM. O. GOODE, Mecklenburg County

[*Constitutional Whig*, March 28, 1832.] Mr. GOODE rose and addressed the House as follows . . .

Mr. Speaker,—in the discussion of this question, gentlemen have indulged in learned reflections, on the evils of slavery in the abstract. They have discussed the morality—the religion of the thing—as though we were deliberating on its original introduction. . . . It is sufficient for me to know, that the thing exists among us—and exists in a form, not to be controlled—that it did exist in this land, and in a form not to be controlled, at the time when our ancestors were called upon to establish our organic law. I know we cannot control the irresistible force of circumstances. . . .

In treating of the effects of slavery, gentlemen have indulged in gloomy representations, of the agricultural condition of the commonwealth. . . . Great injustice has been done this country. Sir, it is in a state of *improvement;* and I call on every member, to reflect on the condition of his own neighborhood, and to respond to this my declaration. A better system of agriculture has been introduced, than existed here ten years since. We do better ploughing. We attend more to the rotation of crops. We attend more to the raising of manures. There is more attention to all the operations of the farm—and there is an obvious improvement exhibited in the whole face of the country. . . . Improvements have been introduced here —first, on the large estates, on which slave labor most abounds; and for the truth of this assertion, I appeal to the candor, experience and observation of every member of this House. . . . Sir, the agricultural product of our State is greater now than it ever was at any previous period; and the gentleman from Brooke, (Mr. Campbell,) who exhibited his tabular statements on yesterday, to show the diminution of our exports, might have learned, had he pushed his inquiry, that the result was effected, not by the diminished quantity of staple reared, but by the depreciation in the price. . . .

. . . Gentlemen in the generosity of their nature have admitted that, the slave is humanely treated. He has an unrestrained abundance of good, substantial, wholesome food—as well for his family, as for himself. He and his family have an ample allowance of comfortable clothing. He is, for the most part well housed. He enjoys many reasonable indulgences. He has set apart for his own use, his garden—or his little field, from which he derives many of the comforts, and even some of the luxuries of life; beyond the reach of the peasantry of other countries. Is he sick? Is his wife, his child, struck down by the hand of disease? He is secure of the best medical aid—of the kindest, the most constant attentions. Is he charged with the commission of crime? He is not entitled to jury trial—because his peers are not good and lawful men—but he is secure of a fair, and public trial. He has two chances to establish his innocence; first before the justice of the peace, and secondly before the courts of police. He is secure of the benefit of counsel, by the humanity of our law—and the commonwealth compels the attendance of his witnesses. . . .

. . . Sir, they [the western people] are graziers, or they are farmers. They want not the slave to follow, or attend their flocks, and herds. As farmers, their demand for labor is but occasional, or periodical; confined for the most part to seed time, and harvest. They are not under the necessity of burdening themselves with the support of the laborer the whole year round: they can procure labor on occasion, in quantities suited to their demand. Hence, their demand for slave labor will not be effectual. It cannot compete with the greater demand, which will exist in the planting country. The man who grows tobacco, cotton and other products of a *plantation,* has a constant, and unremitted demand for a regular force, the whole year round: the operations of his estate must not depend on any precarious supply of labor; it must be certain, and always at command. The planter, therefore, has a greater demand for the labor of the slave, and he will pay more for it, than the farmer, or the grazier. The labor of the slave like every thing else, will go to where it is most useful—will meet the most effectual demand; and our western brethren need not apprehend, that they are to be overrun by our slaves, unless they are willing, and able to pay more for them, than can be obtained in other parts. It was by the operation of this principle, that slavery was banished from the Northern States. The northern people became farmers and graziers—they had no effectual demand for slave labor: it was less useful to them than in the Southern States; it sought the effectual demand of the South; and the number of slaves diminished in the North, until the slave interest, enfeebled and exhausted, was unable to resist the abolition of slavery. Such, sir, I believe, under the dispensation of Divine Providence, will be the course of events here. The superior usefulness of the slaves in the South, will constitute an effectual demand, which will remove them from our limits. We shall send them from our State, because it will be our interest to do so. Our planters are already becoming farmers. Many who grew tobacco as their only staple, have already introduced, and commingled the wheat crop. They are already semi-farmers; and in the natural course of events, they must become more and more so.—As the greater quantity of rich western lands are appropriated to the production of the staple of our planters, that staple will become less profitable.—We shall gradually divert our lands from its production, until we shall become actual farmers.—Then will the necessity for slave labor diminish; then will the effectual demand diminish, and then will the quantity of slaves diminish, until they shall be adapted to the effectual demand. . . .

. . . The thought is constantly recurring to my mind—will the House vote an act of emancipation, without the possibility of compensation? . . . Is it possible for gentlemen to suppose, that this can be accomplished in peace? . . .

Mr. Speaker, if gentlemen have not been hurried away by the heat and ardor of debate—if they cherish the fixed, the immutable purpose of renewing and pressing the consideration of this subject; then, I say, there is no hope of peace, except in a division of **this** great Commonwealth. . . .

(B) SAM. M'D. MOORE, Rockbridge County

[*Constitutional Whig*, Jan. 26, 1832.] Mr. JONES of Elizabeth City, succeeded in a flowing and animated speech in favor of abolition.

[*Constitutional Whig*, March 28, 1832.] Mr. MOORE . . . The construction which he had put upon that declaration, contained in the Bill of Rights, which asserts that all men are by nature equally free and independent, had been denied to be just. It had been affirmed that the principle there asserted, was applicable to men in a state of nature, and not to men in a state of society. . . .

. . . If they had meant to assert the doctrine of the natural equality of men, as applicable only to men in a state of nature, they would have said so expressly. If they had considered it as only applicable to white men, they would have said, that all *white men* are by nature equally free and independent, and not as they did do, that *all men* are so. . . .

It was due to the memory of our ancestors to say, that they had retained their slaves in subjection, not from choice, but from necessity. . . .

An effort had been made to prove that slavery was not inconsistent with the spirit of religion. He was not disposed to go into a minute examination of that branch of the subject, but was prepared to repudiate any religion which would justify slavery. . . . However slavery might be in accordance with the spirit of other religions, certain it was, that it was wholly at variance with that which generally prevails in this country, and which teaches the humblest individual to look upon all men as equal in the eye of his Creator. . . .

THIRTEENTH DAY, WEDNESDAY, JANUARY 25, 1832

(For parliamentary movements on January 25 see pp. 29, 32-33.)

(A) PHILIP A. BOLLING, Buckingham County

[*The Speeches of Philip A. Bolling*, p. 6.] MR. BOLLING rose and said . . .

. . . [p. 8] Those gentlemen who hug slavery to their bosoms, "and roll it as a sweet morsel under the tongue," have been very lavish in their denunciations of all who are for stirring one inch on this subject. They had not hesitated to class all the friends of reform, without any sort of discrimination, with Garrison and Loydd [*sic*]. What sort of resemblance is there between the free and manly discussion of a subject, by freemen, the representatives of freemen, addressed to freemen, and the under-handed attempts of incendiary cut-throats, to sharpen the dagger in the hand of the midnight assassin? . . .

[p. 11] It might seem a needless waste of time for him to point out some of the causes which rendered slave-labor dearer than the labor of a free white man—after the fact had been so fully admitted, notwithstanding he would do so. Why, sir, is slave-labor more expensive, and consequently less profitable than the labor of the white man?

The answer is to be found in the operation of *moral* causes. They have no *immediate self-interest* to act upon them—and you, Mr. Speaker, know something of self-interest. You would not mount your horse and ride twenty miles, to profit another as many dollars; but, sir, you would do so to profit yourself ten shillings. *Self* is the great spring of human action—the great lever that operates on man. This great, this all-powerful motive of action is wanting to stimulate the slave to labor. It fails to operate upon him for good, because he knows his master is bound to provide for him, whether he labors much or little, and whether his master makes little or much. Therefore he is idle and wasteful. He knows, too, that the fetters which shackle him, are only to be struck off by death —he knows that his labor is for life—and that day after day is to bring him the same toil—whether it be on the barren hill, or fertile plain, it is to him the same. He loses nothing by his exertions being wasted upon stingy sterility—he gains nothing, if a generous harvest crowns his labors. He, therefore, can have no motive for improving the soil. . . .

[p. 12] If any man doubts still whether the removal of the slaves would be [p. 13] beneficial, let him turn to the history of man. . . . Let him turn to the trust-deed books, and the saddlebags of the paper-shaver, and he would there learn the fate of but too many who employ slave labor. Most of the slave-owners, sir, are perfectly content, (to use a familiar phrase) if they can make the "tongue and buckle" meet at the end of each year; but very many of them fail in this humble desire. . . .

It may be flattering to the pride of Virginians, to think that a large proportion of the population of the western states are Virginians, or their descendants; but, sir, it creates painful emotions in those who reflect upon that fact as statesmen should reflect. . . . When civil discord shall shake this vast empire to its centre—when the black war-cloud shall lower, and its thunderings be heard from boundary to boundary, and the fierce flash of contest shall play fearfully around us, where, in this dread day of our destiny, in this dark hour of peril, will be Virginia's boasted daughters? Where, then, will be the western states? Where the "great valley of the Mississippi?" They may, perchance, be ranged against her. . . .

[p. 14] However the employment of slave labor might be defended, gentlemen would not, could not justify the traffic in human beings. High-minded men ought to disdain to hold their fellow creatures as articles of traffic—disregarding all the ties of blood and affection—tearing asunder all those sympathies dear to man—dividing husbands and wives, parents and children, as they would cut asunder a piece of cotton cloth. They have hearts and feelings like other men. How many a broken heart—how many a Rachel mourns because her house is left unto her desolate. The time has come when these feelings could not be suppressed—the day would come when they could not be resisted. Slavery was, and had long been offensive to the moral feelings of a large proportion of the community. Their lips had been sealed; but their minds had been unfettered—many had thought, and thought deeply on the subject. This, sir, is a christian community.

They read in their Bibles "do unto all men as you would have them do unto you"—and this golden rule and slavery are hard to reconcile. . . . He did not mean to say, that the population of Virginia was generally characterized by immorality—far from it; but he would [p. 15] say, that slavery always had, and always must produce a great amount of idleness and vice. Where labor is confined principally to slaves, false odium is attached to it—many, who would otherwise be industrious, and laborious, were indisposed to labor—for fear it would bring them down to the level of the slave. He knew that such an idea was a mistaken one, yet it had its effect. If a man had a few slaves, it was hard to get his children to work.

They see the son of a neighbor (who, perhaps, owns fifty or an hundred slaves, while their father might not have more than two or three) playing the gentleman, and taking his pleasure, they desire to do so too—thus a disinclination to labor arises, and indolence and profligacy, too often finish the picture. . . .

His object was not to adopt a rash course,—not to pursue a course, as had been supposed by some who opposed abolition, that would involve a disruption of the good order of society. He did not propose to adopt a system of general emancipation. He only desired to lay the foundation, by disposing of those whom their masters should voluntarily give up, for the total eradication of odious slavery from the good Old Dominion. . . .

(B) WM. N. PATTESON, Buckinham County

[*Richmond Enquirer,* April 3, 1832.] Mr. Bolling having concluded his second address in favor of Abolition—

Mr. PATTESON of Buckingham rose and said . . . It is vain for gentlemen to declare that the people of Virginia expect or desire an act at the hands of this Legislature, abolishing slavery. . . . Gentlemen will be mistaken in supposing that the people of the Eastern portion of Virginia will yield without a struggle, that, for the acquisition of which they have labored and toiled by day and by night, and that, too, when many of the most clamorous against them, were slumbering in comfort, in ease and in peace. . . . He stood here, not as the advocate of slavery as an abstract proposition. No—that is not the question for us to decide. . . . Mr. Speaker, said he, my colleague has drawn a picture of the waning fortunes and blighted prospects of Virginia as the results of slavery, to which he could not subscribe. He believed there was none; for Virginia, he could acknowledge no inferiority to any portion of the world, however favored in point of intelligence or the moral elevation of the character of its citizens. . . . Your Legislative enactments cannot ride in triumph over the Constitution and laws of the land. You cannot 'abate' slave property as a 'nuisance,' as my colleague and others seem to believe, until you abate its holders—and that you cannot do, until God abates their strength. . . .

(C) SPENCER M. BALL, Fairfax County

[*Constitutional Whig,* March 13, 1832.] Mr. BALL said . . . and whilst I am up, I must revert to a remark made a few days since by the gentleman from Norfolk. That gentleman, sir, with a prophetic eye, looking through the vista of an hundred years, presented to your imagination a scene truly appalling. He asked you, with the evidence of the sincerity of his convictions beaming in his countenance, when the bonds which bind this vast confederacy together shall be severed, and the Northern and Eastern States march their armies into Virginia, the frontier border of the South, where will be your resources, with this dangerous population in your bosom? The same argument was made by the gentleman from Rockbridge, and ably answered by the gentleman from New Kent.—I shall, therefore, only say in addition—your resources will be found in the valor and patriotism of the sons of the heroes who fought the battles of the Revolution—unless by a hard and grinding oppression, you drive them from the land of their fathers. I pray God, sir, this prediction may never be verified; and that this Union, which stands a proud monument of the wisdom that formed it, having thus far successfully resisted intestine commotion, and foreign invasion, may remain firm as our native hills, until time shall be merged in eternity. . . . I shall not attempt to argue the abstract question of slavery. Abundant evidence has been exhibited to this House to prove the horrors of slavery as it exists in Virginia are all ideal. Notwithstanding this, I would support any practicable scheme of manumission, provided you obtain the consent of those who alone have a right to dispose of their property as they may think fit. . . .

(D) JOHN S. GALLAHER, Jefferson County

[*Constitutional Whig,* March 13, 1832.] *Substance of Mr.* GALLAHER's *Remarks upon the subject of the Abolition of Slavery.*

Mr. SPEAKER . . . Those who are *slave-holders,* may feel themselves fully at liberty to advocate some movement upon this subject. —As a *non-slave-holder,* I feel bound to hesitate, and to oppose *any* legislative action at this time [see p. 116]. . . .

Mr. Speaker, as an individual, reared with feelings of abhorrence for slavery in all its forms and modifications—if it depended upon my word, (society being prepared for it,) the shackles should fall from every slave in the Universe. And if sustained by my constituents, and entrusted with a place in this House, to express *their* will, I should glory in the privilege of being allowed to vote for its total extinction.

But, sir, I do not stand here to advance *individual* feelings or opinions on this head; or to say what I would do as a citizen. I stand here, as the representative, in part, of a large *slave-holding* interest—of men who have confided to me a guardianship over what they deem their sacred rights—men who have generously reposed confidence in me, notwithstanding my apparent want of identity of interest with them in this particular. . . .

APPENDIX B

List of Delegates, Their Votes and Slaveholdings
(Classified by Sections)[1]

TIDEWATER

				Voting, January 25, 1832[5]			
Delegate[2]	From	Per Cent of District Negro (Slave & Free)[3]	Number of Taxable Slaves Owned by Delegate[4]	Postponement: A Slavery Measure[6]	Preston's Amendment: An Antislavery Measure[6]	Bryce's Preamble: Moderate Antislavery Compromise[6]	Committee Report, with Bryce's Preamble: Moderate Antislavery Compromise[6]
Ball, Spencer M.....	Fairfax.........	46.8	0	Aye	No	No	No
Brown, John T......	Petersburg......	58.7	1	Aye	No	No	No
Carter, Chas. S.....	Prince Wm.....	45.0	21	Aye	No	No	No
Carter, Robert W....	Richmond & Lancaster....	50.9 58.8	52	Aye	No	No	No
Chandler, John A....	Norfolk........	45.4	4[7]	No	No	Aye	Aye
Cobb, Jeremiah.....	Southampton...	59.1	14	Aye	No	No	No
Crump, John C......	Surry..........	59.7	22	Aye	No	No	No
Dabney, Benj. F.....	King William...	67.8	7	Aye	No	No	No
Dickinson, Wm. W.[8]	Caroline........	63.4	43				
Drummond, John P..	Accomack......	43.2	4	No	Aye		
Fisher, Miers W.....	Northampton...	58.6	3	Aye	No	No	No
Grinalds, Southey...	Accomack......	43.2	5	Aye	No	Aye	Aye
Halyburton, Jas. D..	Charles City & New Kent....	67.6 59.9	10	Aye	No	No	No
Hargrave, Jesse.....	Sussex.........	67.6	9	Aye	No	No	No
Harvey, Thos. H....	Northumberland.	49.3	8	Aye	No	No	No
Harwood, Archibald R......	King and Queen.	59.5	19	Aye	No	No	No
Hooe, John.........	King George....	61.3	5	Aye	No	Aye	Aye
Hudgins, Houlder...	Mathews & Middlesex....	47.9 54.7	15[9]	Aye	No	No	No
Jones, Alexander W..	Elizabeth City & Warwick.....	46.5 59.7	4	No	Aye	Aye	Aye
Jordan, Jas. C......	Isle of Wight...	52.2	9	Aye	No	No	No
King, Miles........	Norfolk Borough	47.7	5	No	No	Aye	Aye
Land, Jeremiah T....	Princess Anne...	44.8	?[10]	Aye	No	No	No
Leigh, John P.......	Norfolk........	45.4	13[11]	No	No	Aye	Aye
Mayo, Robt. A.[12]...	Henrico........	55.1	11	No	Aye	Aye	Aye
Moncure, Thos. G...	Stafford........	49.0	?	No	No	Aye	Aye
Newton, Willoughby.	Westmoreland ..	55.8	29	Aye	No	No	No
Patteson, Wm. A. ...	Chesterfield.....	58.6	6	Aye	No	No	No
Powell, Rob't D.....	Spottsylvania...	57.8	1	No	No	Aye	Aye
Ritchie, Archibald...	Essex..........	65.3	26	Aye	No	No	No
Roane, Wm. H......	Hanover........	59.8	?[13]	No	No	Aye	Aye
Rutherfoord, John...	Richmond City .	51.7	5	No	No	Aye	Aye
Shands, Wm........	Prince George...	63.3	9	Aye	No	No	No
Sheild, Robert......	York & Jas. City-Wmsbg.........	60.2 66.6	15	Aye	No	No	No
Smith, Thos........	Gloucester......	59.3	41[14]	Aye	No	No	No
Spencer, Thos.......	Greensville.....	70.4	36	Aye	No	No	No
[Tod, Charles[15].....	Caroline........	63.4	29]				
Webb, Richard D....	Nansemond.....	56.4	3	Aye	No	No	No
[Williams, John G.[16].	Henrico........	55.1	3][17]				
Total for Tidewater		56.2	..	25 10	3 32	11 23	11 23

(Notes to this table on page 114)

TIDEWATER (Notes)

¹ The above classification of counties and towns into the four sections, Tidewater, Piedmont, Valley, and Trans-Alleghany, follows the division used in the census of 1830 as recorded in the 1831-32 *House Journal*, Doc. 21. Those counties formed between the taking of the 1830 census and the election of members to the 1831-32 General Assembly are classified with their major parent counties. The geographical classification here used differs somewhat from that made by Morgan Poitiaux Robinson in his *Virginia Counties: Those Resulting from Virginia Legislation* (Virginia State Library, *Bulletin*, Vol. IX, Nos. 1-3, Richmond, 1916). The older arrangement of counties, though imperfect from a modern interpretation of the natural divisions, is retained because it was the basis for the generalizations concerning population made by the 1832 debaters.
² List of delegates from the 1831-32 *House Journal*.
³ Compiled from census of 1830 as given in 1831-32 *House Journal*, Doc. 21. The counties for which the percentage of blacks is not listed are those formed after the taking of the 1830 census.
⁴ The number of taxable slaves owned by each delegate has been determined from the Personal Property Books (MSS, Va. State Library), 1831. Slaves under twelve years of age were not taxable. The question mark (?) indicates that the delegate's name was not discovered in the Property Books. Where Property Books other than the 1831 series have been used, that fact is indicated in special footnotes.
⁵ The voting of Jan. 25, 1832, is recorded in the 1831-32 *House Journal*, pp. 109-110; *Richmond Enquirer*, Jan. 26, 1832 (with correction of Jan. 28, 1832); *Constitutional Whig*, Jan. 28, 1832.
⁶ These generalizations concerning the character of the various votes should be used with care. Wood of Albemarle, obviously with the slavery group, opposed postponement. He was willing to meet the issue then and there. Several of the compromisers, those who voted against Preston's amendment but who favored Bryce's preamble, voted with the slavery group on postponement. Robt. Gillespie and Jacob Helms, vigorously antislavery as may be seen in their acceptance of Preston's amendment, believed Bryce's preamble and the completed report too mildly antislavery and accordingly refused to accept them. As already stated, Preston's amendment was the clearest antislavery declaration presented as a motion.
⁷ From 1830 Personal Property Book.
⁸ William W. Dickinson, in lieu of Chas. Tod, died during session.
⁹ From 1832 Personal Property Book.
¹⁰ Jeremiah T. Land's son, Peter Land, listed one slave in the 1831 Personal Property Book.
¹¹ From 1830 Personal Property Book.
¹² Robt. A. Mayo, in lieu of John G. Williams, declared ineligible.
¹³ Wm. H. Roane remarked in the debate that he was a "considerable" slaveholder.
¹⁴ The Property Book lists "Thos. Smith, merchant" as owning forty-one slaves and "Thos. Smith" as owning none. It has been assumed that of these two Gloucester County Smiths the wealthier was the delegate.
¹⁵ Chas. Tod died during session. See note 8, above.
¹⁶ John G. Williams declared ineligible. See note 12, above.
¹⁷ Property Book lists "John Williams."

PIEDMONT

Delegate	From	Per Cent of District Negro (Slave & Free)	Number of Taxable Slaves Owned by Delegate	Voting, January 25, 1832			
				Postponement: A Slavery Measure	Preston's Amendment: An Antislavery Measure	Bryce's Preamble: Moderate Antislavery Compromise	Committee Report, with Bryce's Preamble: Moderate Antislavery Compromise
Adams, Isaac	Patrick	25.7	10				
Anderson, Hezekiah R.	Nottoway	70.7	14	Aye	No	No	No
Banks, Linn	Madison	53.6	21	Aye	No	No	No
Bolling, Philip A.	Buckingham	60.9	16	No	Aye	Aye	Aye
Booker, Richard	Amelia	70.2	9	Aye	No	No	No
Broadus, Edmund	Culpeper	49.9	5	Aye	No	No	No
Brodnax, Wm. H.	Dinwiddie	61.6	26	Aye	No	No	No
Bruce, James C.	Halifax	53.9	69	Aye	No	No	No
Bryce, Archibald, Jr.	Goochland	62.8	20	No	No	Aye	Aye
Cabell, Joseph C.	Nelson	53.9	47	Aye	No	No	No
Caldwell, Sam. B. T.	Loudoun	29.3	2[18]	No	Aye	Aye	Aye
Campbell, Robert	Bedford	45.0	12	Aye	No	No	No
Chilton, Mark A.	Fauquier	50.4	10	Aye	No	No	No
Cordell, Presley	Loudoun	29.3	3	No	Aye	Aye	Aye
Daniel, Wm., Jr.	Campbell	50.9	0[19]	Aye	No	No	No
Davis, Thos.	Orange	55.9	13	Aye	No	No	
Dupuy, Asa	Prince Edward	64.3	28	Aye	No	No	No
Garland, Samuel M.	Amherst	51.3	1[20]	No	Aye	Aye	Aye
Gholson, Jas. H.	Brunswick	65.8	16	Aye	No	No	No
Goode, Wm. O.	Mecklenburg	63.5	7	Aye	No	No	No
Gravely, Peyton	Henry	42.8	0	Aye	No	No	No
Hale, Sam	Franklin	34.8	16	Aye	No	No	No
Knox, Alex. G.	Mecklenburg	63.5	0	Aye	No	No	No
Marshall, Thos.	Fauquier	50.4	45	No	No	No	Aye[21]
M'Ilhaney, Jas.	Loudoun	29.3	5[22]	No	Aye	Aye	Aye
Miller, Thomas	Powhatan	68.8	22	Aye	No	No	No
Pate, Edmund	Bedford	45.0	5	Aye	No	No	No
Patteson, Wm. N.	Buckingham	60.9	6[23]	Aye	No	No	No
Pendleton, John S.	Culpeper	49.9	5	Aye	No	No	No
Poindexter, Nicholas J.	Louisa	59.9	11	Aye	No	No	No
Randolph, Thomas J.	Albemarle	53.7	36	No	Aye	Aye	Aye
Richardson, John D.	Charlotte	63.4	26	Aye	No	No	No
Rives, Wm. M.	Campbell	50.9	?	No	No	Aye	Aye
Shell, John E.	Brunswick	65.8	0	Aye	No	No	No
Sims, Wm. D.	Halifax	53.9	1	Aye	No	No	No
Stillman, Geo.	Fluvanna	48.6	0	Aye	No	No	No
Street, John T.	Lunenburg	62.5	12	Aye	No	No	No
Swanson, Wm.	Pittsylvania	43.6	13	Aye	No	No	No
Wilson, Allen	Cumberland	65.3	25	Aye	No	No	No
Witcher, Vincent	Pittsylvania	43.6	10[24]	Aye	No	No	No
Wood, Rice W.	Albemarle	53.7	4	No	No	No	No
Woods, Wyley P.	Franklin	34.8	3	Aye	No	No	No
Total for Piedmont		53.8	..	31 10	6 35	8 33	9 31

[18] Caldwell owned the two slaves in partnership with Wm. Hough.
[19] Although Wm. Daniel, Jr., is listed as a nonslaveholder, Judge Wm. Daniel is listed as owning twenty-seven slaves.
[20] Besides this one slave, Garland as "Trustee" listed twelve slaves.
[21] For Thomas Marshall's change of vote see p. 32.
[22] Jas. M'Ilhaney owned the five slaves in partnership with Aaron Scatterday.
[23] There is listed a "Wm. Patterson" with one slave and a "Capt. Wm. Patterson" with six slaves. It has been assumed that this "Capt. Wm. Patterson" was Delegate Wm. N. Patteson.
[24] Slaves held in name of Vincent Witcher & Son.

VALLEY

Delegate	From	Per Cent of District Negro (Slave & Free)	Number of Taxable Slaves Owned by Delegate	Voting, January 25, 1832			
				Postponement: A Slavery Measure	Preston's Amendment: An Antislavery Measure	Bryce's Preamble: Moderate Antislavery Compromise	Committee Report, with Bryce's Preamble: Moderate Antislavery Compromise
Anderson, Wm......	Botetourt......	27.9	0	No	Aye		
Bare, Samuel......	Shenandoah....	14.6	0	No	Aye	Aye	Aye
Berry, Henry......	Jefferson.......	34.7	3	No	No	Aye	Aye
Brooke, Robert S....	Augusta........	24.4	?	No	Aye	Aye	Aye
Bryce, Jas. G.......	Frederick.......	33.3	?	Aye	No	Aye	Aye
[Byrne, Henry A.[25]	Morgan........	6.5	1]				
Cameron, Andrew W.	Bath..........	30.1	20	No	Aye	Aye	Aye
Carskadon, Thos.....	Hampshire.....	13.1	?	No	Aye	Aye	
Carson, Wm........	Shenandoah....	14.6	3	Aye	No	No	No
Cline, Joseph.......	Rockingham....	13.9	12	No	Aye	Aye	Aye
Faulkner, Charles J..	Berkeley.......	20.9	1	No	Aye	Aye	Aye
Gallaher, John S.....	Jefferson.......	34.7	1	Aye	No	Aye	Aye
Good, William......	Berkeley.......	20.9	2[26]	No	Aye	Aye	Aye
Hiner, Harmon.....	Pendleton......	8.3	0	No	Aye	Aye	Aye
M'Cue, John.......	Augusta........	24.4	4	No	Aye	Aye	Aye
M'Dowell, Jas.......	Rockbridge.....	26.5	4	No	Aye	Aye	Aye
M'Mahon, Wm......	Rockingham....	13.9	6	No	Aye	Aye	Aye
Moore, Sam. M'D...	Rockbridge.....	26.5	3	No	Aye	Aye	Aye
Mullen, John.......	Hardy.........	20.4	5	No	No	Aye	Aye
Persinger, John.....	Alleghany......	22.0	0	No	Aye	Aye	Aye
Poston, Elias.......	Hampshire.....	13.1	0	No	Aye	Aye	Aye
Robertson, Wm. M..	Page..........	....	1[27]	No	Aye	Aye	Aye
Smith, John B. D....	Frederick.......	33.3	?[28]	Aye	No	No	No
Wilson, Geo. W......	Botetourt......	27.9	0	No	Aye	Aye	Aye
Wood, Wm.........	Frederick.......	33.3	1	No	Aye	Aye	Aye
Total for Valley.....	....	22.7	..	4 20	18 6	21 2	20 2

[25] Henry A. Byrne, ejected, having no freehold. Since there was no substitute, the Valley section is listed in this table with twenty-four instead of twenty-five delegates which it received under the 1829 Constitution.
[26] The two slaves are listed as property of "Wm. Good & Son."
[27] From 1832 Personal Property Book.
[28] Two John Smiths are listed, both slaveholders, one owning one slave and the other four. No John B. D. Smith is on the record.

TRANS-ALLEGHANY

Delegate	From	Per Cent of District Negro (Slave & Free)	Number of Taxable Slaves Owned by Delegate	Voting, January 25, 1832			
				Postponement: A Slavery Measure	Preston's Amendment: An Antislavery Measure	Bryce's Preamble: Moderate Antislavery Compromise	Committee Report, with Bryce's Preamble: Moderate Antislavery Compromise
Allen, Jas...........	Lee............	9.8	1	No	Aye	Aye	Aye
Billingsly, Francis...	Monongalia.....	3.4	0	No	Aye	Aye	
Campbell, John C....	Brooke.........	3.8	0[29]	No	Aye	Aye	Aye
Crockett, Charles L..	Wythe..........	18.2	7	No	Aye	Aye	Aye
Erskine, Henry......	Greenbrier......	13.6	7	No	Aye	Aye	Aye
Fitzhugh, Sam. H....	Ohio...........	3.6	0	No	Aye	Aye	Aye
Gilliland, John......	Pocahontas.....	9.6	0[30]	No	Aye	Aye	Aye
Gillespie, Robt......	Tazewell.......	14.6	0	No	Aye	No	No
Hail, Lewis.........	Grayson........	6.7	5[31]	No	Aye	Aye	Aye
Hart, Joseph........	Randolph......	7.5	1	No	Aye	Aye	Aye
Hays, Sam. L.......	Lewis..........	3.0	1	No	Aye	Aye	Aye
Helms, Jacob.......	Floyd..........	....	11	No	Aye	No	No
Henry, Wm. G......	Monongalia.....	3.4	1	No	Aye	Aye	Aye
Jessee, Archer.......	Russell.........	10.6	0	No	Aye	Aye	Aye
Johnson, William....	Harrison.......	5.7	0	No	Aye	Aye	Aye
Keller, John........	Washington.....	18.1	0	No	Aye	Aye	Aye
[Kelly, John W.[32]...	Monroe........	9.8	0]				
Kilgore, Hiram......	Scott..........	6.0	0	No	Aye	Aye	Aye
Lawson, Anthony...	Logan..........	4.6	1	No	Aye	Aye	
M'Coy, John.......	Tyler..........	2.8	1	No	Aye	Aye	Aye
M'Culloch, Thos.....	Washington.....	18.1	0	No	Aye	Aye	Aye
Morris, Isaac.......	Wood..........	14.4	0	No	Aye		
Parriott, John.......	Ohio...........	3.6	0	No	Aye	Aye	Aye
Preston, Wm. B.....	Montgomery....	16.9	0	No	Aye	Aye	Aye
Smith, Nehemiah....	Mason & Jackson......	11.6	0[33]	No	Aye	Aye	Aye
Snidow, Wm. H.....	Giles...........	9.7	?	No	Aye	Aye	Aye
Spurlock, Wm.......	Cabell..........	10.5	0	No	Aye	Aye	Aye
Stephenson, John G..	Nicholas & Fayette......	3.6	0	No	Aye		
Summers, Geo. W. ..	Kanawha.......	19.2	0	No	Aye	Aye	Aye
Vawter, John H.[34]..	Monroe........	9.8	0	No	Aye	Aye	Aye
Williams, George I...	Harrison.......	5.7	0	No	Aye	Aye	Aye
Zinn, Wm. B........	Preston........	3.0	0	No	Aye	Aye	Aye
Total for Trans-Alleghany.............		9.9	..	0 31	31 0	27 2	25 2

[29] No John C. Campbell is listed in the Property Book. However a "John Campbell" and a "Dr. C. John Campbell" are listed as owning no slaves. It has been assumed that Delegate John C. Campbell owned no slaves.

[30] Although John Gilliland's name appears in the 1830 and 1832 Personal Property Books with no slaves listed, he made no tax returns for 1831.

[31] "Capt. Lewis Hail" is listed as having five slaves. "Lewis Hail, Jr." is listed as owning none. It has been assumed that the delegate was "Capt. Lewis Hail."

[32] John W. Kelly was declared unduly elected. See note 34.

[33] "I. & N. Smith" are listed with various properties but with no slaves. No Nehemiah Smith as such is listed. It has been assumed that Nehemiah Smith owned no slaves.

[34] John H. Vawter, in lieu of John W. Kelly, declared unduly elected.

SUMMARY

Section	Number of Delegates	Per Cent of Section Negro (Slave & Free)	Number of Taxable Slaves Owned by Delegates	Voting, January 25, 1832							
				Postponement: A Slavery Measure		Preston's Amendment: An Antislavery Measure		Bryce's Preamble: Moderate Antislavery Compromise		Committee Report with Bryce's Preamble: Moderate Antislavery Compromise	
				Ayes	Noes	Ayes	Noes	Ayes	Noes	Ayes	Noes
Tidewater........	36	56.2	455	25	10	3	32	11	23	11	23
Piedmont.........	42	53.8	574	31	10	6	35	8	33	9	31
Valley............	24[35]	22.7	66	4	20	18	6	21	2	20	2
Trans-Alleghany...	31	9.9	36	0	31	31	0	27	2	25	2
Total............	133	....	1,131	60	71	58	73	67	60	65	58

[35] See note 25.

INDEX

This index does not include names of those delegates who are mentioned only in Appendix B, "List of Delegates, Their Votes and Slaveholdings," pp. 113-118. For additional references to Virginia counties see page numbers under names of various delegates.

"A.B.C.," a pseudonym, 43

Abolitionists, Northern, decline of Southern antislavery sentiment attributed to, 51; incendiary literature published by, 66-67; mentioned, 44-45; Nash Humane and Slave Protecting Society condemns, 42; people not converted by, 6; slavery debate speeches adopted by, 53-54; Southampton Insurrection blamed on, 5-6. See Garrison, William Lloyd; Northern States; Walker, David

Adams, John Quincy, informed of slavery debate, 41; on significance of Dew's *Review*, 49

Agricultural reform, evidences of, 24, 106. See Ruffin, Edmund; Virginia, economic decline of

American Colonization Society, book to aid, destroyed, 55 n.; charters ship, 13; defeat of bill to further work of, 33-35; Dew attacks program of, 49; Harrison defends program of, 49; idealism in, 12; optimism of, in 1831, 13; organized, 11; support of, after 1832, 53. See Colonization.

American Union for the Relief and Improvement of the Colored Race, an antislavery society, 52 n.

Antislavery movement, of Revolutionary era, 9-11. See Abolitionists; Slavery; Slaves

"Appomattox." See Leigh, Benjamin Watkins

Artisans, white, jealous of free Negroes, 12. See Nonslaveholders; Slaveholders, small; Yeomanry

Augusta County, Va., antislavery petitions from, 105

"Bacon's Quarter Branch," a pseudonym, 44.

Ball, Spencer M., extracts from speech of, 111-112; speech of, mentioned, 57, 61; votes and slaveholdings of, 113

Baltimore, Md. See Maryland

Banks, Linn, speaker of House of Delegates, 17; votes and slaveholdings of, 115

Baptist Church, racial friction in, 7. See Churches

Berry, Henry, extracts from speech of, 22, 98-100; speech of, mentioned, 59-60; votes and slaveholdings of, 116

Bible, antislavery arguments based on, 94, 97, 110; proslavery arguments based on, 24, 44, 47-48, 90; referred to, 86

Bledsoe, Albert T., proslavery writer, 52

Blount, Dr., slaves of, remain loyal, 3

Bolling, Philip A., defeated for reelection, 45; extracts from speeches of, 64-65, 108-110; speeches of, mentioned, 57, 59, 61, 67-68; votes and slaveholdings of, 115

Booker, Richard, speech of, mentioned, 57; votes and slaveholdings of, 115

Brodnax, William H., as chairman of select committee, 17-18; extracts from speech of, 70-72; praised by *Enquirer*, 38; speech of, mentioned, 57, 59-60, 74-75, 80, 83, 93; votes and slaveholdings of, 115

Brown, John T., Dew confirms arguments of, 48; extracts from speech of, 88-92; speech of, mentioned, 21, 24, 46, 59-60, 93-94, 96; votes and slaveholdings of, 113

Bruce, James C., extract from speech of, 72-73; speech of, mentioned, 59-60, 83; votes and slaveholdings of, 115

[119]

Bryce, James G., compromise preamble of, 32, 38, 88, 113-118; extract from speech of, 61; speech of, mentioned, 59; votes and slaveholdings of, 116
Burke, Edmund, praised by Leigh, 44
Burr, Aaron, trial of, 14

Cabell, Joseph C., identified with ultraconservatives, 36 n.; votes and slaveholdings of, 115
Calhoun, John C., Duff Green's friendship for, 41-42; spirit of, in Pryor's address, 55; Van Buren's nomination as minister defeated by, 50
Camp meeting, Southampton County farmers attend, 3
Campbell, John C., extracts from speech of, 104-105; speech of, mentioned, 28, 60, 106; votes and slaveholdings of, 117
Chandler, John A., extracts from speech of, 87-88; speech of, mentioned, 59-60, 111; votes and slaveholdings of, 113
Children, evil effect of slavery on, 22, 85; of slaveholders, shun labor, 110. *See* Education.
Churches. *See* Baptist Church; Bible; Camp meeting; Methodist Church; Negro preachers; Negroes, religious instruction of; Quakers; Religion
Clay, Henry, motion of, for tariff modification, 39
Coke, Richard, Jr., Congressman from Virginia, 40-41
Colonization, Federal support of, suggested, 25-26, 40, 72, 79-80; Maryland bill for support of, passes, 40; Virginia bill for support of, defeated, 33-35. *See* American Colonization Society; Free Negroes; Negroes; Slavery; Slaves
Compromise of 1850. *See* Wilmot Proviso
Connecticut, literacy in, 86; population increase in, 91. *See* New England; Northern States
Cooper, Dr. Thomas, teacher of John B. Floyd, 47 n.
Cotton States, attitude of, towards slavery debate, 43; demand for slaves in, 51-52, 107; legislation in, to restrict domestic slave trade, 5, 23, 51, 91-92; prosperity of, after time of slavery debate, 52. *See* Slave trade, domestic; South; *names of various states*
Craig, Robert, Congressman from Virginia, 41
Credit system, slaveholders involved in, 65, 109

Daniel, Wm., Jr., extracts from speech of, 73-74; speech of, mentioned, 59-60; votes and slaveholdings of, 115
Declaration of Independence, mentioned, 39; philosophy of, 10, 20-21, 63-64, 66. *See* Natural rights of man
Delaware, mentioned, 5; population increase in, 91
Dew, Thomas Roderick, author of proslavery essay, 46-49; essay of, mentioned, 52; friend of N. B. Tucker, 53; later career of, 52; represents reaction to antislavery movement in Virginia, 51
Dodd, William E., on Dew's *Review*, 48
Domestic slave trade. *See* Slave trade, domestic

Education, general lack of, in slaveholding states, 86; lack of, among children of nonslaveholders, 64; of Negroes attacked by proslavery group, 42; in North, referred to, 77-78; relative inferiority of Virginia in, 81; slaveholders accused of neglecting a public system of, 24, 69. *See names of various colleges*
Emerson, Ralph Waldo, 21

Faulkner, Charles James, age of, 15 n.; antislavery resolution presented by, 17; career of, 15; Dew refutes arguments of, 48; extracts from speech of, 22, 74-78; speech of, mentioned, 59-60; votes and slaveholdings of, 116
Fauquier County, Va., antislavery petitions from, 105

INDEX

Federal Government, attachment of North to, 78; Dew blames, for depression, 48; Floyd on, 15; plans for obtaining purchase and colonization money from, 25-26, 48, 72, 79-80. *See* Tariff

Fitzhugh, George, proslavery author, 52-53

Floyd, John (Governor of Virginia), alarmed at temper of debate, 37; during Southampton Insurrection, 3, 5, 7; favors antislavery measures, 13, 18; influenced by Dew, 47; nephews of, in House of Delegates, 15, 18, 27; official message of, 15-16, 50; possibly influenced by South Carolinians, 47 n.

Floyd, John B., son of John Floyd, 47 n.

Fortress Monroe, activities of soldiers from, 3, 5

Fisher, Miers W., moves reference of Floyd's message to select committee, 15-16; votes and slaveholdings of, 113

Free Negroes, defended by newspaper writer, 44; emigrate from Southampton County, 13; legal privileges of, restricted, 35; Pennsylvania fears influx of, 39 n.; rapid increase of, 10; removal of, suggested, 12, 15, 18, 25, 33-34, 68, 72, 79-80, 82, 89. *See* American Colonization Society; Colonization; Negroes; Slavery; Slaves

Friends. *See* Quakers

Gabriel Insurrection, 10

Gallaher, John S., extracts from speech of, 112; speech of, mentioned, 57, 61; votes and slaveholdings of, 116

Garland, Samuel M., extracts from speech of, 23, 92; speech of, mentioned, 26-27, 59-60; votes and slaveholdings of, 115

Garrison, William Lloyd, abolitionist, 6, 44, 71, 108. *See* Abolitionists, Northern

Georgia, laws of, to curb domestic slave trade, 12-13. *See* Cotton States; Milledgeville, Ga.

Gholson, James H., extracts from speech of, 24, 65-68; quoted by abolitionists, 53-54; speech of, mentioned, 24, 26, 46, 57, 59-60, 75, 77, 83, 96; votes and slaveholdings of, 115

Goode, William O., Dew confirms arguments of, 48; extracts from speeches of, 27, 61, 105-107; inquires concerning progress of select committee, 18; moves to reject Quaker petition, 16, 17 n.; re-elected to House of Delegates, 45; referred to, 83; resolution of, to discharge select committee from consideration of proposals for abolition, 18-19, 78; speeches of, mentioned, 24, 46, 59, 61

Goodloe, Daniel R., influence of slavery debate on, 42 n.

Gray, Thomas R., editor of Turner's *Confessions*, 4 n., 6

Green, Duff, condemns slavery debate, 41-42; reprints Dew's *Review*, 48

Halyburton, Jas. D., speech of, mentioned, 57, 104, 111; votes and slaveholdings of, 113

Hamilton, James (Governor of South Carolina), 5, 13

Hanover County, petitions from, 16-17, 87. *See* Quakers, petition from

Harrison, Jesse Burton, writes antislavery essay, 49

Hayne, Robert Y., on effect of protective tariff, 39

Helper, Hinton R., influenced by slavery debate, 23

Henry, Patrick, grandfather of William H. Roane, 15, 21; opposition of, to slavery, 10

"Higher law" doctrine, an early edition of, 26-27. *See* Slaves, as property

House of Delegates of Virginia, elections to, in 1832, 45; geographical distribution of membership in, 14; groups in, on a basis of slavery opinion, 29; slaveholders in, 14; *Whig* on specific and implied declarations of, 36; young men in, 14, 15 n.; votes and slaveholdings of members of, 113-118; voting in, on slavery questions, 29-35. *See* Select committee on colored population; Virginia

Indiana, New Orleans shipping port for, 100. *See* Western States
Insurrections. *See* Slave insurrections
Intemperance, causes cruelty to slaves, 64; slavery the indirect cause of, 63. *See* Liquor
Internal improvements, defeat of bill for, 33 n.; general measures for, checked by large slaveholders, 69; relative inferiority of Virginia in, 81; sectionalism causes dispute over, 9; slavery a cause of dissension over, 24

Jackson, Andrew, democracy of, 8; Kitchen Cabinet of, 41
"Jefferson," a pseudonym, 45
Jefferson, Thomas, Dew attacks principles of, 48; grandfather of T. J. Randolph, 15; as inspirer of Randolph plan, 73, 95; Leigh attacks actions and principles of, 44; natural rights of man defined by, 20; opposes slavery, 10; passing of spirit of, 55-56; Summers accused of plagiarizing, 22, 44; theory and practice of, contrasted, 26, 83. *See* Declaration of Independence; Randolph, Thomas Jefferson
Jenifer, Daniel, Congressman from Maryland, 40
Jones, Alexander W., speech of, mentioned, 57, 108; votes and slaveholdings of, 113

Kennedy, John Pendleton, 53
Kentucky, New Orleans shipping port for, 100. *See* Western States
King, Rufus, antislavery proposal of, revived, 26
Knox, Alexander G., extracts from speech of, 24-25, 83-84; re-elected to House of Delegates, 45; speech of, mentioned, 24, 46, 60; votes and slaveholdings of, 115
Knoxville, Tenn., newspaper of, favors antislavery movement, 42. *See* Western States

Labor, manual, made dishonorable because of slavery, 22, 39-40, 63, 79, 85, 110
Lee, Richard Henry, opposes slavery, 10
Lee, Robert E., 14
Leigh, Benjamin Watkins, Dew confirms arguments of, 48; opposes antislavery movement, 44-46
Liquor, mentioned, 3, 44, 72, 104. *See* Intemperance
Louisiana, laws of, to curb domestic slave trade, 12-13. *See* Cotton States; New Orleans, La.
Lynching of Negroes, in Southampton County, 4, 21, 35-36

McDowell, James, Jr., age of, 15 n.; career of, 15; Dew refutes arguments of, 48; explanation from, 104; extracts from speech of, 21, 27, 100-104; leader of liberals, 18; speech of, mentioned, 22, 24, 59-60, 111; votes and slaveholdings of, 116; and Wilmot Proviso, 54 n.
Madison, James, officer of American Colonization Society, 13
Marshall, John, attempts to protect Cherokees, 50; father of Thomas Marshall, 14-15, 41; favors Federal aid in antislavery plans, 41 n.; Leigh acquainted with, 44; officer of American Colonization Society, 11, 13; tells Adams of slavery debate, 41; and trial of Aaron Burr, 14
Marshall, Thomas, changes vote, 32; extracts from speech of, 22-23, 78-80; favors obtaining Federal aid in antislavery program, 26; member of House of Delegates, 14-15; speech of, basis of Harrison's essay, 49; speech of, mentioned, 57, 59-60; views of, reflected by John Marshal, 41; votes and slaveholdings of, 115
Maryland, interest of, in slavery debate, 40; legislature of, passes colonization bill, 40
Mason, George, natural rights of man described by, 20; opposes slavery, 10

INDEX 123

Massachusetts, population increase in, 91. *See* New England; Northern States

Mecklenburg County, Va., citizens of, condemn antislavery movement, 43; conservatives from, re-elected, 45

Methodist Church, attacked by proslavery group, 42. *See* Churches

Milledgeville, Ga., newspaper of, on slavery debate, 43. *See* Georgia

Miscegenation, newspaper writer on practice of, 44

Mississippi. *See* Cotton States

Moore, Samuel McDowell, age of, 15 n.; extracts from speeches of, 20-21, 62-64, 108; leader in debate, 18 n.; speeches of, mentioned, 22, 57, 59, 61, 66, 71; votes and slaveholdings of, 116

Nash Humane and Slave Protecting Society, a proslavery organization, 42

Natchez, of U. S. Navy, 3

Natural rights of man, referred to, 24, 47-48, 66, 81, 84, 93, 108. *See* Declaration of Independence, philosophy of; Jefferson, Thomas.

Negro preachers, Floyd indicates danger from, 15; legislation to silence, 35; Turner numbered among, 3

Negroes, anthropological characteristics of, 81; antislavery group accused of desiring to enfranchise, 45; contentment of, 85; density of, in Virginia, 9, 30; insurrection of, in Southampton County, 3-8; peaceful nature of, 48; preponderance of, in eastern Virginia, 11-12, 23, 51-52, 65, 96; religious instruction of, 53; removal of part, recommended, 72, 79-80. *See* American Colonization Society; Colonization; Free Negroes; Lynching of Negroes; Miscegenation; Negro preachers; Slave codes; Slave insurrections; Slave trade; Slavery; Slaves; Virginia

New Bern, N. C., agitated by Southampton Insurrection, 5. *See* North Carolina

New England, nature of early settlers in, 81. *See* Northern States

New Jersey, population increase in, 91. *See* Northern States

New Orleans, La., exports from, 100. *See* Louisiana

Newton, Willoughby, extracts from speech of, 27, 97-98; speech of, mentioned, 60; votes and slaveholdings of, 113

Niles, Hezekiah, on cause of Southern depression, 40

Nonslaveholders, attitude of, towards slavery, 38 n.; destructive influence of slavery on, 22, 64, 77, 96-97; Gallaher numbered among, 112; in House of Delegates, 14, 113-117; patrols made up principally of, 86, 97; as possible voters under Randolph plan, 70-71. *See* Pioneer farmer; Poor whites; Yeomanry

Norfolk, Va., Floyd on fright of, 7; newspapers of, reprinted in Northern States, 38

Northern States, Congressmen from, quote McDowell, 54 n.; economic causes for abolition of slavery in, 107; Green on politicians from, 48; interest of, in slavery debate, 38-40; invasion of Virginia by, prophesied, 111; orators of, identify slavery with low tariff policy, 50; publication of incendiary literature in, 66-67; Southern poverty caused by, 91; sympathetic understanding of, 6-7, 71; Virginia compared with, 23, 67, 69, 77-78. *See* Abolitionists, Northern; New England

North Carolina, agitated by insurrection, 5; attitude of, towards antislavery movement, 42; men from, patrol Southampton County, 3; Walker once a resident of, 10

Nullification. *See* South Carolina; Tariff

Ohio, New Orleans shipping port for, 100; people of, interested in slavery debate, 38. *See* Northern States

"One-vote legend," error of, 34-35

Overseers, punishment by, 62

Page County, Va., antislavery petitions from, 105

Panic of 1819, effect of, on Virginia, 9, 96

Patrols for control of Negroes, 35 n., 86, 97

Patteson, Wm. N., extracts from speech of, 111; speech of, mentioned, 57, 59, 61; votes and slaveholdings of, 115

Pennsylvania, economic conditions in, 67; New Orleans shipping port for western part of, 100; people of, interested in slavery debate, 38, 39 n. *See* Northern States; Philadelphia, Pa.

Petersburg, Va., fright in, 7; newspapers of, reprinted in Northern States, 38

Philadelphia, Pa., Dew's essay first published in, 46; people of, interested in slavery debate, 38. *See* Pennsylvania

Pioneer farmer, characteristics of, 86

Plantation system, compared with farming system as to labor requirements, 106-107; restricted to eastern Virginia, 8

Pleasants, James H., editor, 4 n., 42. *See* Virginia, press of

Poinsett, Joel R., tells Tocqueville of slavery debate, 43

Poor whites, demoralizing influence of slavery on, 62-63; ignorance of, encouraged by slaveholders, 24, 69; slavery drives away, 64; as tenants, will be forced from land, 63. *See* Nonslaveholders

Post nati plans of emancipation, justified, 77, 87. *See* Randolph, Thomas Jefferson, antislavery plan of

Powell, Rob't. D., extracts from speech of, 73; speech of, mentioned, 59-60; votes and slaveholdings of, 113

Preston, James P., father of William B. Preston, 15

Preston, William B., antislavery amendment of, 19, 29, 31-33, 101, 104-105, 113-118; age of, 15 n.; brief remarks of, 98; career of, 15; extracts from speech of, 28, 82-83; leader of liberals, 18; speech of, mentioned, 59-60; votes and slaveholdings of, 117

Prince William County, petitions from, 73

Pryor, Roger A., Congressman from Virginia, 55

Public lands, income from, a possible aid in antislavery plans, 25-26, 72, 80

Quakers, general antislavery activities of, 9-10; petition from, 16-17, 20, 104-105. *See* Churches; Hanover County

"Quietus," a pseudonym, 43-44

Randolph-Macon College, 52

Randolph, Thomas Jefferson, age of, 15 n.; antislavery plan of, 19, 26, 65, 68-71, 73, 78, 96-98, 102; Dew refutes arguments of, 48; extracts from speeches of, 65, 95-97; member of House of Delegates, 15; re-elected to House of Delegates, 45; speeches of, mentioned, 24, 57-60, 68, 105; votes and slaveholdings of, 115. See *Post nati* plans of emancipation

Reform Bill, English, 50

Religion, literalism in, 56; slavery inconsistent with, 85, 97, 108. *See* Bible; Churches

Representative system, Randolph's plan an attack on, 26, 96-98

Richmond, Va., discovery of incendiary pamphlet in, 10; General Assembly convenes in, 14; interest of, in slavery debate, 37. *See* Virginia

Ritchie, Thomas, disliked by conservatives, 38 n. *See* Virginia, press of

Rives, William M., extracts from speech of, 68-69; speech of, mentioned, 24, 59-60, 95; votes and slaveholdings of, 115

Roane, William H., extracts from speech of, 21, 80-81; member of House of Delegates, 15; presents antislavery petition, 16; remarks of, in 1833, 50 n.; speech of, mentioned, 57, 59-60; votes and slaveholdings of, 113. *See* Quakers, petition from

INDEX

125

Ruffin, Edmund, agricultural reformer, 52 n.; proslavery author, 53
Ruffner, Henry, denounces slavery, 53
Rutherfoord, John, speech of, mentioned, 57; votes and slaveholdings of, 113

Santo Domingo, insurrection in, 51, 65. *See* Slave insurrections
Select committee on colored population, 15-19, 28-29, 32-33, 61, 73, 80, 87, 101, 104-105, 113-118
Shell, John E., extracts from speech of, 24, 94-95; speech of, mentioned, 60; votes and slaveholdings of, 115
Silliman, Benjamin, on antislavery movement of 1832, 40
Slave breeding, 26, 66, 83, 97. *See* Slave trade, domestic
Slave codes, severe nature of, 99; strengthened, 6, 10, 12, 15, 35
Slave insurrections, danger of, 12, 20, 23, 51, 63, 65-66, 98. *See* Gabriel Insurrection; Southampton County, insurrection in; Turner, Nat
Slave trade, domestic, 5, 12-13, 21, 23, 51-52, 63, 68, 75, 110; foreign, 10, 47-48
Slaveholders, in general, 14, 24, 65, 109; large, 38 n., 69, 97; small, 38 n., 69. *See* Slavery; Slaves
Slavery, antidemocratic tendencies of, 69, arguments in defense of, summarized, 24-25; arguments in opposition to, summarized, 20-24; a cause of political differences, 23-24, 69, 78, 103; early movement against, 9-11; economic deficiencies of, 22, 65, 77-79, 85, 100; effect of, on whites, in general, 21-22, 67-68, 85-86; as an evil, in general, 21-22, 40, 70, 73, 77-78, 81, 83-84, 99-100; factors in decline of opposition to, 49-52; happiness incompatible with, 83; historical argument in defense of, 24, 47, 84, 90; immoral influence of, 62-63; manual labor made dishonorable by, 22, 39-40, 63, 79, 85, 110; mildness of, in Virginia, 21, 64,

67, 103, 112; national defense impaired by, 63; plans for abolition of, 10-13, 15-19, 24-27, 29, 31-34, 36, 38, 41, 44, 47-48, 51, 61, 70, 72-73, 76-83, 85, 87-89, 95, 99, 104-105, 110-112; as a theme for public debate, 20, 87-88, 101, 104. *See* Abolitionists; American Colonization Society; Bible; Colonization; Dew, Thomas Roderick; Leigh, Benjamin Watkins; Negroes; Nonslaveholders; Northern States; Slave breeding; Slave codes; Slave insurrections; Slave trade; Slaveholders; Slaves; Southampton County, Va., insurrection in; Virginia; Western Virginia
Slaves, contentment of, 74, 83-84, 90, 93-94, 102-103; cruelty to, 62; ignorance of, 62; immorality of, 62-63; increase of, 91, 96; normal instincts in, 102-103; price of, 20, 51, 61, 68, 70, 96; as property, 26-27, 42, 48, 61, 66, 70, 73, 75-76, 80, 82-83, 87-88, 93, 96, 98-101, 111; punishment of, 62; treatment of, in general, 21, 67, 71, 78, 86-87, 103, 106. *See* Negroes; Slavery
Smith, William A., proslavery writer, 52
Soil exhaustion, in Virginia, 9, 65, 79. *See* Slavery, economic deficiencies of
South, agitated by Southampton Insurrection, 5; economic depression in, 44, 48, 50; political isolation of, 103. *See* Cotton States; *names of various states*
South Carolina, attitude of, on slavery question, 42-43; and protective tariff, 39, 50; relations between Floyd and people of, 15, 47 n.; Virginia accepts conservative philosophy of, 56. *See* Hamilton, James
Southampton County, Va., emigration of free Negroes from, 13; insurrection in, 3-8, 15, 49, 93-95, 103-104. *See* Lynching of Negroes; Slave insurrections; Turner, Nat
State rights, favorite theme of conservatives, 26, 48. *See* Federal Government; Tariff

126 INDEX

Stokes, Montfort (Governor of North Carolina), 5
Story, Joseph, 41
Stringfellow, Thornton, proslavery writer, 52
Summers, George W., accused of plagiarizing Jefferson, 22, 44; age of, 15 n.; extracts from speech of, 20, 22, 26, 84-87; reminiscences of, 51 n.; speech of, mentioned, 59-60; votes and slaveholdings of, 117

Tappan, Arthur, sponsor of antislavery society, 52 n.
Tariff, sectionalism encouraged by controversy over, 7; slavery question confused by controversy over, 39-40, 50; Southern poverty caused by, 39, 41, 48, 91
Tennessee. *See* Knoxville, Tenn.; Western States
Tobacco, better prices of, 52; decreasing emphasis on raising of, 107; mentioned, 37, 42. *See* Agricultural reform; Panic of 1819; Plantation system; Virginia, economic decline of
Tocqueville, Alexis de, informed of slavery debate, 43
Tucker, Nathaniel Beverley, author, 53
Tucker, St. George, father of N. B. Tucker, 53; opposes slavery, 10
Turner, Nat, insurrection led by, 3-8, 41, 94-95, 103-104. *See* Southampton County, Va., insurrection in

University of Virginia, 52

Van Buren, Martin, 50
Vaughan's Tavern, disliked by troops in Southampton County, 4
Virginia, agricultural economy of, east and west, compared, 89; aristocratic character of early settlers in, 81-82; attack on, by North prophesied, 111; constitutional conventions in, 9, 22, 44, 55; early antislavery movement in, 9-11; economic decline of, 9, 22-23, 44, 65, 67, 77, 91, 101, 105-106, 111; emigration from, 23-24, 68, 91, 95, 105, 109; end of depression in, 52; evidences of sectionalism in, 8-9, 16-17, 27-28, 31, 33, 40-41, 50, 53, 55, 69, 74-75, 82, 86, 88-89, 92-93, 96, 99, 113-118; later antislavery movement in, 53; map showing density of colored population in, 30; press of, in general, 12, 14, 17-18, 38, 40, 43-44, 50, 61; prohibits foreign slave trade, 10; relative decline of population in, 11, 91; separation of, suggested, 28, 37, 50, 74, 92, 95, 104, 107; special reasons for lack of commercial development in, 81-82. *See* House of Delegates of Virginia; Northern States, Virginia compared with; Negroes; Slavery; Slaves; University of Virginia; Western Virginia

Walker, David, inflammatory pamphlet of, 6 n., 10; mentioned, 71. *See* Abolitionists, Northern
Walsh, Robert, editor, 46 n.
Warren, of U. S. Navy, 3
Washington College, 53
Washington, D. C., reaction of, to slavery debate, 40-42
Washington, George, opposes slavery, 10
Webster, Daniel, 28
Western States, economic competition from, 9, 107; growth of, 91; interest of, in slavery debate, 42; movement of Virginians into, 95; New Orleans shipping port for, 100; possible danger from, in event of civil war, 109-110. *See* Virginia, emigration from; *names of various states*
Western Virginia, characteristics of pioneer farmer in, 86; New Orleans shipping port for, 100; typical economy of, 89, 106-107; votes and slaveholdings of delegates from, 116-117. *See* Virginia, evidences of sectionalism in; Virginia, separation of, suggested
Wheat, new emphasis on production of, 107. *See* Agricultural reform; Western Virginia

William and Mary College, faculty members of, 10, 46, 52-53

Williams, George I., extracts from speech of, 21, 92-94; speech of, mentioned, 60; votes and slaveholdings of, 117

Wilmington, N. C., erroneously reported destroyed, 5

Wilmot Proviso, quotations from 1832 speeches used in debate over, 54 n.

Witcher, Vincent, motion of, for indefinite postponement of controversial issues, 29, 33, 113-118; votes and slaveholdings of, 115

Wood, Rice W., extracts from speech of, 81-82; opposes postponement and antislavery measures, 29 n., 114 n.; speech of, mentioned, 59-60; votes and slaveholdings of, 115

Women, antislavery petitions from, 16 n.; attend slavery debate, 37, 87-88

Worcester vs. Georgia, 50

Wright, Frances, reformer, 16 n.

Wythe, George, opposes slavery, 10

Yeomanry, injured by slavery, 22, 75, 78. *See* Nonslaveholders; Slaveholders, small; Western Virginia

Historical Papers of the
Trinity College Historical Society
Series XXIV